Does Anyone Here Know God?

Gladys M. Hunt

Does Anyone Here Know God?

Stories of Women Who Do

Zondervan Publishing House
Grand Rapids, Michigan

Does Anyone Here Know God?

Library of Congress catalog card number: 67-11622

First printing . . . . . April, 1967
Second printing . . . . May, 1967

Printed in the United States of America

Grateful acknowledgment is made to the following for permission to use copyright material:

DOUBLEDAY & COMPANY INC.

Excerpts from *Thomas* by Shelley Mydams, copyright © 1965 by Shelley Mydans.

HARPER & ROW, PUBLISHERS, INC.

"Lest We Forget," from *Prayers of Women* by Lisa Sergio.

WILLIAMSON MUSIC INC.

Excerpts from "Some Enchanted Evening," copyright © 1949 by Richard Rodgers and Oscar Hammerstein II.

To my Mother and Father
who first introduced me to God.

ACKNOWLEDGMENTS

I had no idea that writing this book would be such an exhilarating experience when Floyd Thatcher and Mary Ruth Howes, both of Zondervan Publishing House, first suggested the idea to me. I'm indebted to them for not letting me refuse the opportunity, and for all the help they have been since then.

My chief encourager has been my husband, Keith, whose enthusiasm has urged me to leave home and hearth to get the material. His concern, his well-pleased look, and his helpful comments have spurred me on to completion and given me extra cause to thank God for him.

The regular query, "How's the book doing, Mom?" of our fifteen-year-old son, Mark, suggests only part of the loving fellowship of our family over this project.

Two dear friends have been regular helpers: Julie Roseberry, who helped type the manuscript; Geraldine Potter, whose prayers for me accomplished more than I can appreciate. Others, too numerous to mention, have been faithful in this latter ministry for me.

Of course, I am primarily indebted to the women who shared themselves with me so that I could tell you their stories.

GLADYS M. HUNT

FOREWORD

In a society that cries out, "Does anyone here know God?" how refreshing to read these stories of contemporary women who have encountered Christ and have been transformed by His power. As these women have shared their innermost convictions and discoveries, it is apparent that God is real, dependable, loving and caring.

This personal witness of God's power will be like a chain reaction to stimulate believing faith in the heart of every reader.

In a day when it is difficult to find time to read, isn't it a joy to find a book so inspiring and exciting that one can't put it down?

Having read *Does Anyone Here Know God?* I am sure you will want to share it with others.

"Charm is deceitful and beauty is passing, but a woman who reveres the Lord will be praised" (Proverbs 31:30, Berkeley).

MRS. CLIFF ("BILLY") BARROWS

CONTENTS

I

Introduction

WHO'S afraid of God? Eve was. She hid from Him because she was afraid to face this One who knew exactly what she had done and why. She had chosen her own way, tested the authority of God, and then blamed someone else. Guilty and cut off from His presence by sin, she preferred floundering around on her own to meeting Him face to face.

Eve's great granddaughters many times removed have inherited her perplexity. Some, either subconsciously or deliberately, remain ignorant about Him out of fear. They suffer from some kind of cosmic claustrophobia.

Others, more arrogant, assert that they can make it on their own, that they don't need a crutch like God, and they try to stay as far away from Him as they can. They say, "I've lived a good life. Isn't that enough?"

A few meet Him as children and, untainted by sophistication, see Him as He is and never forget. But sometimes even these become scared of His Bigness as they grow older, and try to keep the friendship casual. Which is simply another way of being afraid.

It does seem risky to open up your life to One as Big as God, admitting to Him what He already knows. Hiding behind the cover of our intellectual reasoning and our personal charm seems much safer than standing out in the glaring light of His presence alone and saying, "Here I am,

God. I need you." To say nothing of asking for His friendship.

Being a Christian is not for cowards. God's fellowship is liable to lead a person into "such terribly exciting truth that the stubborn human littleness in us shies off at the merest mention of Him."[1] Fear says it's best to stay on the safe side, giving a slight nod to Him now and again, in case we ever need His power to bail us out of an extreme distress — like a desperately ill child or an unfaithful husband. The trouble is that God remains a stranger, so unknown that you can begin to wonder if He is even real.

God offers to everyone the opportunity to know His reality. He wants to invade our scared human littleness and bring us into a whole new understanding of Himself, of life, or ourselves. He wants us to stop hiding and come out into the open and have our guilt taken care of in the cross of Christ. He wants to invade our lives and let us experience what it means to know Him — a staggering concept!

I don't know what you think of when God is mentioned, but the God I am talking about is the God of the Bible. Sadly misrepresented, God has been caricatured as a celestial computer, an angry judge or a genial white-bearded grandfather. Other people try to shrivel God down to their size and have the arrogance to say, "I cannot conceive of a God who . . ." or "I think God is . . ." All of which is somewhat ridiculous. God is God. Men through the ages have thought they had Him all safely defined and conquered and put the lid on the box, only to turn around and be blinded by a fresh revelation of His greatness and glory. No, we are not the final word on God's godness. If you want to know God, you will find He has revealed Himself in the Bible and in His Son Jesus Christ.

I grew up knowing about God because my mother and father loved Him and talked to Him every day about my brothers, my sister and me. I believed in Him. I believed

---

[1]John Hercus, *More Pages from God's Casebook* (Chicago: Inter-Varsity Press, 1965), p. 15.

God had sent His Son Jesus Christ to die for my sins, and as a young child I told Him that I wanted to be His. I went off to the university believing this, and suddenly found myself in a hostile world without family support. No one I met seemed to believe that God was even important, least of all that they should live under His authority.

As a matter of fact, one of my professors was convinced He was nothing but a myth, an expression of human need. And he set out to lead me into the same freedom from ignorance. "You're too intelligent," he'd say, "to be caught in this stuff you learned at your mother's knee."

He told me many things I didn't know. From his loaded point of view God looked like a pretty stupid idea and the Bible thoroughly unreliable as evidence for any truth. He was a Ph.D., and I was a lowly freshman.

Walking back to the dorm after our conversations together, I would go over the evidence in my mind. (I didn't know another Christian on campus because I hadn't yet discovered a student group called Inter-Varsity Christian Fellowship.) Was God real? How could I know for sure?

I decided simply to ask Him if He were real to take me from childhood acceptance into a convincing adult experience of His reality. In my room I opened my Bible and truths I never saw before stood out as clearly as words spoken aloud by a voice from heaven, and they were for me personally. I told my professor about this, about the verses I read each day. It made him very uncomfortable. Words from the Bible *are* discomfiting to the uncommitted.

My professor was kind, gentle and sincere. He was a good man, as people say. But what he told me in those sessions together were the words of an unbeliever. His thinking and talking began with man and man's sufficiency. I had been brought up to begin with God. And those two are radically different foundations on which to build a philosophy of life.

I hadn't learned yet to ask, "What's your basic premise?" but I found God was putting some other pretty good questions about this man-centered theory in my mind. (How impressed my professor would have been if I had been knowledgeable enough to tell him that his views were anthropocentric!)

The one irrefutable evidence I had was my experience of seeing what faith in God had produced in the lives of others close to me. I thought of my mother and father, of my grandparents and of others I knew who claimed to know and trust God. There was something shining about their lives in comparison to the earthbound approach of my professor. I thought, *What are the hard questions of life that could test a theory? Who has the best answers to guilt? To death? To the unknowns?*

My professor rationalized guilt, and told me tedious facts of progress in understanding the unknown. But when I asked him about death, he was suddenly angry. I knew he had no answer, that he was afraid. And I remembered what I had read about One who walked right through death and who is able "to deliver those who through fear of death were subject to lifelong bondage."[2]

I had seen death close up only once, and what I had seen defied all laws of human tragedy. My aunt, thirty-four years old, three children, a loving husband, dying from cancer by inches. No amount of brainwashing, wishful thinking or myths could have accounted for the quiet confidence and trust I observed in her dying. Nothing but the reality of God. Surely, I thought, this is life's ultimate end, and not to have a workable answer for this is absolute folly.

God didn't blast in on me from outer space with lights or voices or wondrous signs. As I opened my mind to Him and said, "Prove yourself," He did. He became undisputably real to me. I found being a Christian is knowing God through Christ, having a personal relationship, not just believing truths.

Arguments didn't win or lose the case. I just felt the impact of God in my life. I knew He, above all else, was Truth, and what He said was true. I saw my learned pro-

---

[2]Hebrews 2:15, RSV.

fessor as a Ph.D. in English, not in God. And it made a difference. God opened my mouth, He convinced my intellect, and He warmed my heart. I found I was committed to Jesus Christ.

Life has been like that ever since — not filled with sadness or hardness, but a proving of His reality in simpler adventures with Him. He has taken us (*I* became *we* shortly after graduation) from safe, secure and sensible routines into the delight of trusting Him in unlikely places at home and abroad. Yet just saying that shows how easily we underestimate God, for what could be safer or more sensible than relying on an all-powerful God?

Frankly, I can't quite describe the sheer joy of knowing God. That's why I have written this book — in an attempt to let you in on what God does when people open up their lives to Him. My friends help tell the story by telling their own stories. These aren't complete biographies. These chapters are simply answers to the question I believe the world is asking, "Does anyone here know God?"

Don't make the mistake of putting haloes around the heads of these women, and then use their halo as an excuse to avoid evaluating the validity of their experience. Remember, Christianity is for sinners, not for people who are too good to come to God for help. The people in this book are very human. Not one of them has a stained-glass look. They often disappoint themselves and are disappointed by others. In short, they are people like you.

God isn't real to them because they are better or worse than anyone else. He is real to them because they have opened their heart and received Him. God is strange that way. He doesn't force Himself on anyone. Of course, as you read, you'll see that He makes Himself pretty obvious by the power He exerts, but He is always there for everyone, waiting to be asked to come in and take over.

2

Eleanor Whitney

I remember when a monthly women's magazine featured Eleanor Searle Whitney as one of the best dressed women in America. Since that day Eleanor Whitney has been given a new dress — a heavenly dress, if you please. It is the only one that really matters to her now, for it is the garment of salvation, the righteousness of Jesus Christ.

ELEANOR SEARLE WHITNEY has a lot going for her," wrote one columnist after hearing Eleanor speak at the Beverly Hilton. Another wrote: "She hits you with a thundering impact because she is just about the smartest dressed woman you've ever seen. She has a pretty little girl face, dark eyes, dark hair, and is slender and graceful. Mrs. Whitney is a lovely lady, a fireball, an evangelist."

When adjectives fail, reporters refer to her as a "New York socialite, noted for many best-dressed awards, a concert singer, and for seventeen years the wife of multimillionaire Cornelius Vanderbilt Whitney." And all the reporters grab up the fact that she was named best-hatted woman so many times that she was permanently retired to the American Millinery Institute Hall of Fame as the best-hatted member of society. Eleanor takes advantage of this and shows her gold bangle, shaped like a hat, studded with pearls and a diamond on the crown. Then she talks about the tangible and intangible hats a woman is called to wear — wife, homemaker, PTA member, or whatever her role — and how the hat labeled *Christian* is the most important one to wear and affects all the others.

Eleanor does this because something has happened to her. She *is* wealthy, gifted and beautiful, so much so that some women inevitably feel threatened when she walks in the room. But Eleanor is *more* than that. She has become a dynamic child of God, not just in the family, but enthusiastically so. And this is the reason all the reporters are interested, and others come to hear her speak. They thought she had everything without God, and now she comes and exposes the empty desires of their own hearts. They forget to describe what chic thing Mrs. Whitney is wearing, and begin to write down I Timothy 3:5, 6 and Ephesians 2:8, prescribed reading suggested by the speaker.

I first met Eleanor Whitney at a private dinner given by Mr. and Mrs. Herbert Taylor in Park Ridge, Illinois. She is all the things others said about her, but mostly she is simply Eleanor, a woman who knows she has been redeemed by God.

A growing, learning woman, vitally alive, she is frankly excited about knowing God. I found myself wishing she lived down the road from me so we could talk some more. In that evening together she managed nicely to challenge all the guests to a more forthright witness of the reality of God's work in their lives. She minces no words about her own commitment, and when she tells her story, it goes something like this:

Eight years ago, something happened in my life. I had a fresh encounter with God's love, and my entire understanding of what it means to be a Christian was put into a new focus. I had always assumed I was an adequate Christian. I was living a moral, kind, thoughtful, generous life concerned with helping the underprivileged and handicapped, contributing to educational, health and cultural projects. I was living an ethical life and I worked in the church. What else could anyone ask? I found out later I was really an "ethical do-gooder," not a Christian God could use.

I have a rather ecumenical background. A fourth generation Lutheran, I was baptized and confirmed in the Lutheran Church which my great-grandfather founded and built and paid for in Ohio, my home state. My father was an Anglican, born in London. I went to a Methodist college. My family winters in Bradenton, Florida, and since there is no Lutheran church there, I've been a winter Presbyterian. Since I moved to Long Island twenty years ago, I have attended the Episcopal Church. It was through the efforts of a Baptist that I re-dedicated my life to Christ.

But all of this really doesn't matter. The important fact is that today I believe Jesus Christ is God in the flesh and that He died on the cross for me. I have committed my life to Him, and received His gift of forgiveness and Life.

All of my life I have been active in church. Being a singer, I have often attended five services a weekend. One is bound to absorb something from these contacts, and I could quote from the Bible, and I have always prayed. I had everything the world has to offer — homes, apartments, hunting and fishing lodges, cars, yachts, airplanes, horses and stables, possessions and fame. I had no need in my life from outward appearances, but spiritually I was poverty-stricken. I think it was Pascal who said, "There's a God-shaped vacuum in every heart that can only be filled with a relationship to God."

There are lots of ways to try to fill that vacuum. Some try more activities, dedication to charitable enterprises, another trip, another mate, or another bottle of liquor. It works for a while, as long as you don't think too much, or until God breaks through in your life. I had chosen the "do-gooding" routine. Life was very pleasant and seemingly left nothing to be desired.

When I was still a teenager, a college boy and girl visited in my home over a holiday, and asked me if I was a Christian. Of course, I replied in the affirmative; I had been confirmed the year before. They asked, "Well, what did you confirm?" I hadn't confirmed anything; the church confirmed me. I was unaware that I was supposed to have confirmed Christ as my Saviour, Master and Lord by inviting Him to take over my life. I had learned the creeds and become a member of the church, participating actively in its programs.

These collegians, however, explained to me how Jesus had told Nicodemus (in John 3) that although he did good and was sincere, he had to be *born-again spiritually* to get into God's family. They explained that no church can save us, that only Jesus Christ could do that. That is what John 1:12 means: *But as many as received Him, to them He gave power to become a son or daughter of God.*

And so, as a teenager, I made a commitment. I didn't know anyone else who talked about these things. We had no Young Life, Youth for Christ, Inter-Varsity, Navigators, Campus Crusade or any other organization to reach me. My mother was the only *born-again* Christian I knew, and I thought it was "square." With no fellowship and my instruction limited to hearing sermons, I grew up but remained a spiritual baby.

In the summer of 1957, Billy Graham held a Crusade in New York City. Our Episcopal rector encouraged us to go, and I took carloads of friends in from Long Island many times. I was deeply impressed, and each time I would see people thronging forward, I'd think, "Isn't it wonderful! *They* need it."

After attending many meetings of the Crusade, the feeling grew that I had to make a response, too. I wanted to reaffirm my faith in God, to be sure I knew where I was going to spend eternity. Not because I could ever deserve to be with God, but because I knew that Christ gave eternal life to those who trusted Him. Yet when I would start to go forward, I would think of my friends laughing at me, calling me a silly goose, or a holy joe. Or a voice would say, "You don't have to do that. You *are* a Christian," and I would sit tight and not move.

Finally I drove to New York one night all alone. I suppose in my subconscious I must have thought, "Now if I get that funny feeling and want to go forward, I can, and no one will ever know about it." You see I was really too ashamed and timid to let anyone know I loved God and was responding to Him. I knew so little of what He wanted me to be, and I used to think when I saw others go forward, *That's all so emotional, and it never lasts.*

It was emotional. You'll never know how I felt getting up out of my seat and starting down the long involved labyrinth of corridors in Madison Square Garden. I wept my eyes out as if I were a long straying child returning to my Father's home. Ruth Graham, Billy's wife, was my counselor, and I'll always be grateful for the gentle, loving way she understood my need and opened the Bible to show me what it said about the importance of each person making his own relationship to God. God has no grandchildren. Each of us has to do this on our own.

The next morning if anyone had asked me, "What difference will going forward make in your life?" I could never have answered, any more than a newborn baby could answer the question, "Tell me about your birth last night and what you are going to do when you grow up." I only knew that Christ was real to me.

Later I found that several friends of mine had also gone forward at the Crusade and knew as little as I did about the Bible. We knew that we had to know more about God and the place to find out was the Bible. So we started a Bible Class. We were scoffed at in our fashionable Long Island north shore area and all our friends said, "The girls are on a Bible binge!"

It's been a long binge. Our little class has continued to be a source of spiritual feeding for us, and today, eight years later, we have twelve such classes in the area. Many of the scoffers are coming, too, and finding Life. We have a memory verse for each week, and we are learning to pray aloud by having different prayer partners for each week. The group urges its members to have a daily Quiet Time to study the Bible and then we are encouraged to take our turn in leading the discussion. You've no idea what an exciting experience this has been for all of us! It has become the highlight of the week.

Inviting Christ into your heart doesn't mean all your troubles are over. I've had my greatest tragedies since my decision. About a year after I gave my life to God afresh, my whole world exploded and fell apart. My husband of seventeen years insisted on a divorce to marry someone he had known only a few months. I'm sure that the awful heartache of this tragic time would have made me a candidate for the bottle, the psychiatrist's couch, the minister's shoulder, the sleeping pill escape or any other crutch — if I hadn't known Jesus Christ. Imagine being able to go to God's Word and claim words like these for myself, *Let not your heart be troubled, neither let it be afraid. . . . Lo, I am with you always. . . . I will never leave you nor forsake you. . . . All things work together for good to those who love God. . . . My strength cometh from the Lord. . . .* I hung on to God and found He was enough.

I sometimes think Christians are like tea bags. You never know what kind you are until you are in hot water. Then you find out if it works. Jesus told us that we would have tribulations in this world, but to cheer up because He had overcome the world. Just two years ago my lovely twenty-four year old step-daughter died, four months after we discovered she had leukemia. That was hard to take. But I know she took a short-cut to go home to be with God for eternity, while some of the rest of us have to stay here to be tested, to be used, and to be refined. But through it all, we have the inner joy of knowing God.

I had my share of problems before I came back to God, too. Possessions cannot shield you from this. I have had a heart condition all my life, and when I was younger, it curtailed my sports activities. Every time I had an attack I was sure I was going to die. Then the war took a brother. I lost many babies, and when my son was born I was told he wouldn't live either although he eventually overcame his physical difficulties. This is what life is like.

What a tower of strength and inspiration my mother has been to me in this area of faith. Just a short time ago, although well along in age, Mother had to have her left leg amputated mid-thigh because of a circulatory disorder. Before the operation she said, "Darling, it doesn't matter whether I go home to be with my Father on the operating table or a year from now. I know where I'm going to spend eternity. My bags are all packed!"

She has taught me a lot about trusting God. In three days she was up and I took her for a ride in a wheel chair in the hospital corridor. She was home in one week, and a month later she took me to her Bible classes which she regularly attends.

Since I've come to know more of Christ and the Word of God I have had more opportunities to speak of Him than I could ever have imagined. I've spoken about Him literally around the world. A witness testifies about what he knows through personal experience, about something that he saw, or heard, or felt. This is what I try to do in various ways, by lecturing, singing, or in private conversation. I try to be like the woman in the Bible about whom Jesus said: "She hath done what she could."

People invite Eleanor Whitney to speak and come to hear her because of who she is, but they never leave without knowing *what* she is. She has spoken and sung about Jesus Christ at the First Lady's and the President's Prayer Breakfast in Washington, at corporation meetings, at the electrician's union meeting (where she spoke of being properly wired, but not connected to the main power supply), to women's gatherings and men's service clubs of all denominations. On an airplane headed across the country, a businessman will ask, "Who do you work for?" And she will tell him,

"The King." Which invariably arouses his curiosity, and a good discussion about the ultimate issues of life follows.

Eleanor is news wherever she goes. After an interview with Eleanor in her hotel room, a woman reporter was a bit awed. Eleanor had prayed for her, she said, and on the way down the elevator had reached into her carryall, produced a pen and hastily scrawled her name and favorite Bible verses in a small book of selected scriptures called *Living Water* and given it to her. Afterwards the reporter wrote, "She stepped out of the elevator looking like a fashion model, greeted her woman driver and asked her how long she had been a Christian. She doesn't waste a second. I've never met anyone like her. She made me feel I was missing out on something big. Her evangelistic zeal sweeps everything — and everyone before it."

And one bejeweled and bedecked woman was heard to say after hearing Eleanor, "After that luncheon I can get rid of these hurry-up and slow-down pills and make room for this," and she waved a small white Bible before tucking it into her handbag.

Clearly Eleanor Whitney is redeeming the time, and those who meet her know she has found that the secret is living for Jesus Christ.

3

Margaret Barnhouse

Margaret Bell Barnhouse is the wife of the late Donald Grey Barnhouse, well-known Bible teacher and minister of Tenth Presbyterian Church in Philadelphia. The story of her changed life began with a discussion on flying saucers one night in a country club in Florida.

THEY HAD STAYED on for dinner after Doug had finished his golf game at the country club near their home in Florida. Margaret Bell didn't golf, but enjoyed walking the course with her husband. Later, sitting around the club and talking with their friends, the conversation got off on the inevitable subject of flying saucers.

There had been a rash of flying saucer reports in this 1949-50 era, and now the afternoon paper had carried a headline story of one being sighted landing in the Everglades. Someone had even seen strange little men going in and out of it. The topic was thoroughly exploited. One person laughed it off as ridiculous. Another remarked that a flying saucer was mentioned by an eighteenth century writer.

Then one man, who had sat quietly throughout this lively discussion, stunned them all when he drawled out, "I can go you one better than that. Perfect description of a flying saucer in the Bible."

Doug Bell scoffed, "Where?"

"Don't you remember 'the wheel within a wheel ringed round with fire'? Perfect description of a flying saucer."

The conversation went on from there. But the comment about "the wheel within a wheel" piqued Doug's curiosity. On the way home he asked Marge, "Where is that about the flying saucer — you know, 'the wheel within a wheel' "?

"What do you mean, where?" asked Marge.

"Where in the Bible?" True to his nature, Doug was hot on the trail for the facts like an old hound dog. Doug Bell always seemed to have a series of fascinating hobbies which he explored with diligent enthusiasm until he had exhausted their possibilities. Then he found a new interest and went into that with the same thoroughness. He was currently on a whodunit binge, and this conversation had given him a clue that needed to be tracked down.

"Don't we have a Bible somewhere around?" he asked Marge. She supposed that somewhere among her belongings was the one she had been given when she joined the church at eight years old. At home, Doug persisted about that Bible and she dug through her treasures and finally found it. Neither of them knew where to look for a "wheel within a wheel," so whodunit Doug Bell started reading at the beginning in Genesis to find it.

This begins the story of how God finally broke through into the life of Margaret Bell (now Barnhouse.) For forty years she had lived a self-satisfied self-righteous life. She had grown up in a loving home in a small town near Albany, New York, enjoying the security of belonging to the right family, knowing the right people and attending the right school. After her graduation from Bryn Mawr College she married the right man, had the right home and belonged to the right set. Doug rapidly climbed the success ladder.

When it came to religion, she took their two children to Sunday school, and read the Sunday newspaper while she waited for them in the car. Sometimes she and Doug went to church and criticized the sermon if it wasn't intellectual enough. It wasn't that she didn't believe in God; everyone did that unless they were way out. She just was casual about Him. The Bells were simply a nice, ethical, sociable couple.

When Marge had the first of three bouts with tuberculosis early in their marriage, she had time to think. She was sent to Saranac Lake for "cure" and for the first time she suspected that her life might not be as fulfilled as she would like to think it was. The frenzied activity of her life as a civic leader had put her flat on her back. Maybe there *was* a missing ingredient. But after each "cure" she went back to the same routine and thoughts about God receded from her consciousness.

Then they moved to Florida to enjoy life in the land of sunshine with their two children, ten and twelve. Doug had semi-retired and they spent long hours boating, fishing and relaxing at the country club. Now he had gotten this bug about finding the "wheel within the wheel" and was reading the Bible straight through — and finding it fascinating. He had gotten only to the third chapter of Genesis and already he was saying, "This is great, Marge. Listen to this!" And he would read her the passage.

Marge had somewhat the same reaction she had when she was a little girl, visiting her grandmother in Kentucky. She and her young brother had been playing checkers on the floor when her grandmother, seated in the old-fashioned platform rocker reading her Bible, had gasped a little schoolgirl cry of delight. Hopping up the children had asked, "What's the matter, Grandma Lew?" "Listen to this," Grandmother had said, and then had read something from the New Testament to them, her face glowing. Marge couldn't see anything so exciting about that and went back to checkers. Now Doug was sounding like Grandmother, and Marge couldn't understand him either. It didn't seem all that great to her.

Doug's enthusiasm didn't wane as he waded through the Pentateuch and on into Jewish history. He'd say, "This is terrific! Why don't the ministers give it to us straight?" He didn't touch another whodunit. By the time he got to Ezekiel he had forgotten all about "the wheel within the wheel." And in three months he was through the Bible.

But something had happened to him; he didn't know what. He was restless, searching. He kept asking Marge all kinds of questions about God which she couldn't answer. Doug had always said that he had been made to go to church and Sunday school by his Methodist mother and father and that was why he didn't go now. (A few years later, when he said this, Dr. Donald Barnhouse asked him whether he had stopped taking baths for the same reason!) But suddenly he wanted all the information he didn't have.

One day he said, "You know, Marge, I've learned something from the Bible and it has really got me worried. We haven't been giving what we should to God. We've just been giving the kids a nickel for Sunday school, and the Bible says we ought to give a tithe."

"What's a tithe?" asked Marge, suspiciously.

"Ten per cent of your year's income which belongs to God."

"You're joking, Doug. That's too much." Marge was horrified that he should consider such an amount with their present income. But Doug was serious. He figured out the amount and wrote a check for the year's tithe. Marge could do little but go along with the idea. Doug decided not to give it to the big downtown church which they occasionally attended, but to a struggling mission church on their end of town. He made an appointment with the minister, explained the situation and gave him the check. However, he made a few definite stipulations: *Don't ask me to join the church, don't put my name on a list. Don't call me, I'll call you.*

Shortly thereafter Doug went on a business trip to New York and visited the book section at Macy's department store.

He told the librarian that he wanted to know all about religion and would like a copy of everything they had on the subject.

She queried, "Everything?" and took him to an enormous room lined with hundreds of books. "Sir, this is just a sampling of what we have on religion."

Doug gulped and left instructions that a sampling of a sampling be sent to him at his home in Florida.

This was too much for Marge. Doug's religious binge was just too expensive. First the tithe and now a hundred dollars' worth of books. To make matters worse, Dug ripped up most of them after he read them. They often retired early and read in bed since Marge needed an unusual amount of rest. Now, instead of the mystery stories, Doug read these books. He would finish one and say, "This is ridiculous. This isn't what the Bible says at all," and he would tear it apart and toss it in the wastebasket.

Marge would clutch for the book, wondering if it cost $5.95 or $8.50, and say, "Well, let me at least read it before you throw it away."

"It isn't worth your time," he would say. And soon his analytical mind had clicked off the next book with the same result. When he was finished, only seven or eight books remained in one piece on the book shelf. He could have been led off into all kinds of tangents by this reading, but he wasn't. In retrospect, Marge sees that God gave him unusual discernment.

Their first Sunday at home after their vacation that year, the Bells decided to drop in on the service of the mission church. They met in the school library for lack of their own building, and Doug, to his surprise, found a number of his buddies attending the service, too. This made him feel at home right from the start, and both of them recognized that there was something different about this group.

The minister had a slight speech impediment and was not easy to listen to. But the hymns of the church were sung with such joy by these people — *maybe,* thought Marge, *I have been missing something all these years.* After the service everyone was very cordial and one of Doug's friends told him about the special speaker they were having that evening and invited him to come back. So Doug agreed, and the Bells, who almost never went to church, found themselves going twice on one day and to the mid-week prayer service as well!

Marge had never been in a prayer meeting in her life and didn't especially like the idea of going now. *Prayer meetings were for fanatics,* she thought, *for the overly emotional who moaned and carried on.* But this was quite different. Here they were in the school library with their friends, and people were talking to God as if He were real, as if they knew Him and as if He were there. She had never had an experience like it. Doug lapped it up. This is what he had been looking for. Next Sunday the Bells were back for two services, and the mid-week prayer service again — all of which must have astounded the minister who had been told not to bother them or to expect them to show up at church.

Church attendance became a habit, and eventually Marge was asked to teach a junior high Sunday school class. *This I can do,* she thought. She had been feeling left out of things because she just couldn't seem to whip up enough interest and fervor to keep up with Doug's spiritual interests. So she studied the lesson quarterly with utmost care, and without discernment. She shudders now to realize what she must have taught because the material questioned everything from the virgin birth to the Resurrection and cast doubt on all the basic fundamentals of the faith. "But," says Marge, "I got on fine because no one else knew what was happening." The obvious enthusiasm for God among these people still made her a bit uneasy.

Everyone got excited when the minister announced plans for Youth Week at the church. A young minister who was well-known as an athlete was coming from Kentucky to speak primarily to the young people. The way people talked and prayed about this sounded a bit hysterical to Marge. She thought the safest thing would be to volunteer to serve refreshments. This way she could hear what the speaker said but be out of the way. So she squeezed oranges with one ear glued to the kitchen door. By the end of the week, fifteen young people (her own two children included) had made a firm commitment to Christ and were simply glowing. It was more than Marge could understand.

Sunday night the young man, tall and handsome, spoke to the parents, mincing no words. Parents, he said, often hindered their children. At the end of his message he gave an invitation to parents to give their lives to God and join their children in Christian commitment. Marge had never heard this done before.

Now Doug was a business man, not sentimental nor easily swayed. In fact, he was downright sane and sensible. But suddenly Marge was aware that her husband, who had been sitting over by the wall, was on his feet weeping, pushing past everyone's knees toward the aisle, and going to the front! Marge stared in astonishment. Doug's best friend stood and went forward, too. Then three more of his friends, all members of the same hard drinking crowd. *What has come over them,* Marge thought. *Here is my husband, humbling himself by kneeling in public with his head in his hands — weeping!*

Then the young minister said, "If any of you are on praying ground, come up and join these people and pray them through." Now Marge didn't know what "praying ground" or "praying through" was exactly. Maybe it was just southern talk. But she did believe she was a very good, very nice person and doubted that she would have any trouble at all getting into heaven. Whatever had happened to her husband she didn't know, but at least she could go stand with him in his distress. So she got herself up and went down the aisle and put her hand on Doug's shoulder. He was heaving with sobs. Marge still didn't understand, but she patted him comfortingly, yet feeling terribly left out and rationalizing that she was probably too intellectual for this sort of thing. Afterwards when Doug got to his feet, his face was shining — a completely different look. Suddenly everyone was crying, laughing and hugging each other. Marge was acutely uncomfortable.

The next morning when everyone in this small southern town stopped at 10:30 for the coffee break, the drug store was simply humming. The men pushed tables together and the group listened as the five men told what had happened to them. Everyone was talking about God and the change in these men. Marge thought, *Well, Doug is a nicer person for all of this. The fuss will soon pass over.*

But it didn't pass, and the coffee breaks turned into a men's Sunday morning Bible class, with Doug as the teacher. These men literally turned the town upside down. So vital was their group that they were eventually asked by the prison warden if he could parole any man with rehabilitation potential to this group's custody.

Doug felt he had to know more about God. A friend's mother lived in Sarasota and Doug had heard she was a good Bible teacher. So the five men took their wives (one of whom shared Marge's confusion at the turn of events) and visited this woman. She hadn't talked to them for any time at all before she realized that they knew very little. "I have just the book for you to study," she told them; "*Teaching the Word of Truth* by Donald Grey Barnhouse."

"Who is he?" Marge asked innocently.

"Why, darling," the Bible teacher replied in her southern-soft voice, "he just happens to be the most famous Bible expositor in the whole United States, and in my opinion, he's the greatest in the world!"

Marge thumbed through the book. "Why, this is for children!" she objected.

"My dear, that's just what you all are right now in understanding," was the reply. "The preface says this is 'For young Christians of any age.' "

The Bible teacher agreed to teach the class which began meeting weekly on Friday nights. Soon other men in Doug's social group came to these classes and they returned with their friends. Before three years were up, anywhere from eighty to over one hundred and fifty came each Friday night.

As they arrived for the class meeting, the teacher gave out slips of paper with Bible verses for each to look up ahead of time to save them the embarrassment of not knowing their way around in the Bible. Marge says she could have told you act and line from Shakespeare, but she didn't know where to find the book of Hebrews in the Bible. They hadn't taught her that at Bryn Mawr, and so naturally she looked in the Old Testament!

Shortly after they had begun these studies, on a December Friday night, it was her turn to read a Bible verse, and the reference was Isaiah 64:6. In her best Bryn Mawr accent she read, "We are all as an unclean thing and all our righteousnesses are as filthy rags." As soon as she realized what she had read, she did a double take, and looked again at the verse.

Marge didn't hear the rest of the lesson. She was too busy arguing with God about all the good things she had done. "But I couldn't find any place where God took into account what I did. He didn't seem to care about committees, Sunday school classes, refreshments, Girl Scouts, or any of my good works. That was hard to take," Marge says now. "I didn't come to God all at once; I fought every inch of the way. As I stood at the kitchen sink peeling onions one day I thought, *This is me. I come off by layers.*"

Marge doesn't remember exactly when it happened, but there came a time when she knew that Doug really did know the answer. Her own children and the children in her Sunday school class knew the truth better than she did and were asking embarrassing questions. She often cried out, "God, help me. I want to do the right thing, but I'm all mixed up." Finally she admitted defeat and said, "Lord, you win. I can't fight anymore. Now what do I do?"

God gave her His answer. He told her, *Believe.* It was like falling in love; she was swept off her feet by the Lord Jesus Christ. She couldn't put into words how she felt, but she knew she wanted God and He had accepted her.

Sometimes she had some reservations about the implications of this, but basically she was committed to Jesus Christ. She expressed this openly when their church had revival services, a thing she had never heard of either. She got her proud, intellectual self out of her seat and up to the altar where she wept and prayed, no longer thinking of her reputation.

By this time the group of men Doug was leading really had made an impact on the community. Marge had thought Doug's enthusiasm would blow over, but this was the real thing. The men's faces, once hard and selfish and closed, were now soft, warm and interested in others. Instead of five men out drinking in their boat, now Doug took his friends and there were often five men out praying in a boat. That was enough to shock any town. Then the wives began to meet and study the Bible together — without a teacher. They simply used material their Friday class teacher suggested and took turns leading the study. Every woman who came had the experience of digging into the Bible for herself, and they found it was exciting.

Having used Dr. Barnhouse's book on Friday nights, this core group of Christians became interested in him as a person. Someone had heard that he had a radio broadcast and that it was heard on the east coast of Florida. When they wrote to find out why it couldn't be heard on the west coast, they were told that there were no funds to take on another station. So they raised the money to have the broadcast come to western Florida. The broadcast series began in Romans and they ate it up.

Then the Bible teacher heard that Dr. Barnhouse was having a series of meetings in the Miami area. She shared this news with the men, and they wasted no time contacting the Evangelical Foundation in Philadelphia, which handled Dr. Barnhouse's speaking schedule, to see if he would come to speak on the west coast. When he agreed, they hired the Civic Auditorium in Sarasota for $1000, got out publicity and filled the place. No one told them they couldn't do it, and it never occurred to them to doubt that these meetings would be a success.

When Donald Barnhouse appeared on the platform to speak, Marge Bell, for one, was surprised. She had expected an older man, somewhat ethereal looking. Instead she saw this big, earthy looking man who looked as though he had slept in his clothes and needed more sleep still. (They found out later he had and he did!) When he got up to speak, he began by looking up and down every row, fixing each person in his photographic memory — an action they later discovered was his habit. He spoke on "The Scales of God," and the group was electrified by a kind of preaching they had never heard before. Frankly, Marge was torn between anger and admiration — she felt he was aiming right at her with his remarks and she resented being so thoroughly exposed. Several others thought the same thing.

After the meeting the Bells and their friends took Dr. Barnhouse out for dinner. Nothing delighted him more than spiritual thirst in people. They fired questions at him thick and fast, and he answered from the Scriptures. What a week that was — a veritable feast for learning.

The following week Dr. Barnhouse had a series of meetings in Tampa, and the whole group trooped up to hear him again. After the meetings Dr. Barnhouse would join them and answer more questions. He recognized that Doug Bell was as ripe for learning as any man he had ever met. Doug couldn't get enough. This was like going to seminary to have these hours with this great teacher.

When the meetings at Tampa were over, Doug remarked that he wished Dr. Barnhouse could stay one more week. Dr. Barnhouse said, "Well, is there any reason why you couldn't arrange your affairs and travel with me to the next place?"

This was too good an opportunity to miss. Doug decided he could handle his business by phone, and he went with Donald Barnhouse to his next preaching series. Driving in the car Dr. Barnhouse taught this eager student what he wanted to know about the Bible. At the end of the next week, Doug called Marge. "Marge, this is simply terrific. You've got to get some more of it. Can't you come out and join us? Can't you make some arrangements for the children?"

Marge could. In fact, Doug's parents had just come for a

long visit and were willing to stay with the children. She flew out to Arkansas and together they spent six weeks traveling with Dr. Barnhouse, learning and absorbing, as he taught from a different book of the Bible in each city.

Discussing it as they rolled along in the car together, he would drive them into the Scriptures to find their own answers. It was a marvelous experience for two new Christians. Donald Barnhouse and Doug became very close friends, and warmly appreciated each other. Dr. Barnhouse knew a good man when he saw one, and later asked Doug to join the Board of the Evangelical Foundation.

Marge now had more knowledge and understanding of biblical truth than she ever could have dreamed possible. But the more she learned, the more uneasy she became about the depth of her own commitment. She and God knew that she still had some reservations.

About this time *South Pacific* was popular on Broadway and everyone was singing the hit tunes from that musical. At home, working around the house, the words of "Some Enchanted Evening" would flit through her mind. Without thinking, within a few minutes, she would be humming "Beneath the Cross of Jesus," and the two tunes seemed to be fighting for her attention.

Marge says, "Have you ever been in a crowd and felt someone was staring at you, and you wondered what was wrong, yet you were hesitant to turn around and look back? Suddenly as I was singing 'Some Enchanted Evening' I realized that is what I was doing to Jesus Christ. He had His steady gaze on me because He wanted to get through to me, and my back was turned. I wouldn't look around. I knew in my heart I'd been swept along by Doug's enthusiasm for God and that God wanted my heart in a way I hadn't yet given it. I looked very good to my friends, but I knew how I looked to God. I knew all the things that kept me from being wholly His.

"Finally I couldn't stand holding out any longer. So I thought, *All right, I'll turn around look Him full in the face and admit it.* And do you know, He wasn't looking at me to criticize me. He was looking at me because He *loved me.* I was overwhelmed.

"These words came to me, all rolled into one.

> Some enchanted evening you may see a Stranger, . . .
> When you feel Him call you across a crowded room;
> Then fly to His side and make Him your own
> Or all of your life you may dream all alone.
> Once you have found Him never let Him go,
> Once you have found Him never let Him go.[1]
> Beneath the cross of Jesus I fain would take my stand,
> The shadow of a mighty rock within a weary land.

"Not very orthodox perhaps. But my heart was won completely by a glimpse of His great love."

Another year passed. The Bells could scarcely believe how different their whole life was now — just three years since Doug first became excited about "the wheel within the wheel." They lived differently, they thought differently, they were different because they *knew* God. Trusting Him, opportunities were unlimited. Doug became involved in helping the North Africa Mission, whose leadership he had met through Dr. Barnhouse.

Doug and Marge had planned to spend a year together in North Africa — Tangiers — now that their daughter was graduating from high school. Doug was going to help solve a monetary exchange problem for the Mission. He had everything packed away because he was going on a journey. He did go on a journey, only it was a different one than they had planned. The night of Carolyn's graduation Doug, forty-six years old, was stricken with a heart attack, and two days later he was gone. Before he died, Doug said, "Marge, if I go home to heaven, be sure to call Dr. Barnhouse."

---

[1]From *"Some Enchanted Evening,"* copyright © 1949 by Richard Rodgers and Oscar Hammerstein II. Williamson Music Inc., New York, New York, publisher and owner of publication and allied rights for all countries of Western Hemisphere.

The funeral was more like a triumphal entry than an ordinary funeral. Marge couldn't get over how knowing the Lord Jesus Christ had changed this experience of death for her. The men so dear to Doug were all there, and at the end of a magnificent message, the congregation stood and sang the Doxology together. That was a long way to come in three years.

After the funeral Marge remembered Doug's words to get in touch with Dr. Barnhouse. He was so insistent, almost as if he felt his spiritual father was a rock to which she could tie in her grief. So Marge sent a message through a mutual friend and within minutes Dr. Barnhouse was on the phone, strengthening her in the loss of his dear friend.

The night of the funeral God had led Marge to read, *Trust in the Lord with all your heart and lean not on your own understanding. In all your ways acknowledge Him and He will direct your paths — Proverbs* 3:5, 6. In the months ahead she found her paths directed toward Donald Barnhouse in a new way. Eventually she became the wife of this dynamic man.

At heart Marge has always been an adventurer. She was game for Doug's adventure when he retired at thirty-nine to Florida on considerably less income than he made as a company president. She had had an exciting adventure with Jesus Christ in the last three years of Doug's life. Now God took her into a new adventure with Donald Barnhouse.

Dr. Barnhouse had been a widower for about ten years. He had a great capacity for sharing and endless curiosity about new information. He was the kind of man who loved exploring nature as much as exploring a book. Life with him was never dull. On their Barchdale Farm outside of Philadelphia, Marge would hear him call and run to find out what urgent thing he needed, only to find him in the rose garden saying, "Marge, look at this rose. Isn't it the most exquisite thing you have ever seen!"

Marge was ideally suited for her new role, and delighted to share in Donald Barnhouse's life and ministry. She was the sounding board for many of his ideas, and she gave him a few in return. In 1960 after six and a half enriching years together, Dr. Barnhouse also went home to heaven.

On one occasion, expressing her panic at the thought of death one day separating them, Marge had said, "I don't know what I would ever do without you, Donald!"

Donald Barnhouse had replied with loving fierceness, "Listen, Marge. You lean on God and I'll lean on God and then no matter what happens to either of us, we'll each have our Leaning Post."

Today a beautiful gray-haired, blue-eyed Marge Barnhouse has a ministry in her own right. She has a great capacity for loving, and God has given her people to love. She simply shares herself and what God has taught her.

There's a freshness about Marge, a genuineness that reflects the confidence of a right relationship with God. That's what God does for the person who trusts Him.

4

Leja Messenger

Once a Russian baroness with a three-hundred-room castle, Leja Von Wolfe-Leudinghausen de Torinoff Messenger now has a new title and a new wealth. She met God in a remarkable way just before the Revolution swept away all of the security she had known in life.

THE MISTRESS of the castle was eight years old and an orphan. Three hundred rooms of dark, cold loneliness, the castle stood outside Riga in Latvia, near the Prussian border, surrounded by vast farm lands tilled by hundreds of tenants attached to the land. By story-book standards the castle was fit for a princess. It had come down to Leja Von Wolfe-Leudinghausen through her grandmother who had been one of the princesses of the Romanoff dynasty. Leja's father, the baron, was brought home dead when she was three, and five years later death severed her close attachment to her beautiful mother. The tragedy and desolation of a young child's life hangs in these few sentences.

Today Leja Von Wolfe-Leudinghausen de Torinoff Messenger lives in a five room walk-up apartment in old Grand Rapids, Michigan. They are a charming, cozy five rooms because she has made them that way, but with amusement at the contrast she recounts the tale of the wearisome three hundred rooms, each done exclusively in baroque or renaissance or whatever the period might be.

"My life has been in periods, too," she says, "almost as if I have had three separate lives." She is so obviously happy. Nothing could matter less to Leja Messenger today than castles or houses or lands.

The baroness, Leja's mother, was an unusual woman of high birth and noble ideals. She was only a young woman when she died, but she planted and nurtured ideas and values in her daughter that Leja remembers today. On one occasion, sitting out in the garden in the warm June sun together just before she died, the baroness told her daughter, "Nobility is a great responsibility. Lineage and title have no meaning," she said, "unless you also have nobility of heart and mind."

Just at that moment, the old gardener came with a gift of fresh cut flowers, something her mother especially enjoyed. After he had gone, the baroness told Leja, "That dear man, the gardener, is more noble than many princes and consorts I have known."

At her mother's death, Leja was utterly alone. Her father's sister, who didn't like children in general and Leja in particular, came to manage her affairs. She was a cold efficient woman (bringing with her three governesses to take charge of Leja), and shortly thereafter doubled Leja's fortune. As nearly as she can figure in rubles, her annual income must have been in the area of a million dollars.

Today Leja Messenger asks children, "Would you like to have a million dollars and live in a huge castle?" They all eagerly say yes, but when she tells her story the envy disappears. For Leja had no brothers or sisters or playmates or friends. During the three years following her mother's death, she neither saw nor heard another child.

Leja learned to amuse herself, developing her natural sense of humor. Without this, she might have broken mentally. The target of her amusements was her governesses. Three of them! Leja says she has never found anyone else who had more than one governess at a time to torment them. But she had three — one English, one German, one French. The delight of her day was to find some new mischief to confound their propriety. Especially was she on the warpath against the English governess and the English language. Imagine a language where an *r* follows a *w*. Or the *th* combination. It made Leja furious. With every other language she could speak using her lips and her tongue, but in English she even had to use her teeth!

Youth is without pity, and so Leja was without pity towards her English governess, Miss Greene. She said everything wrong on purpose. She pulled all the tricks she knew. Miss Greene was clearly the strictest and most competent of the governesses, and relentlessly hammered at Leja to get her to comprehend and speak the English language. Today Leja believes that God gave her Miss Greene, to prepare her for the day when the English language was her only friend as she arrived in America. But then the learning process was not so pleasant, and no one could have convinced a young Leja that her English governess was heaven-sent!

On one particularly trying day, Miss Greene reached the end of her patience — and came to the "you-say-it-right-or-I-quit" point. This frightened Leja. Afraid both of her demanding aunt and the possibility of a new governess, she stammered out an apology, and also produced a clear, distinct series of "*wh*en, *wh*at, *wh*y, *wh*ere, *wh*o, *th*rough, *th*ough, *th*is, and *th*at." She had been difficult, she admitted, and called in her French maid, whom she had been teaching English, as proof of her pranks. "From that day on," says Leja, "Miss Greene and I and the English language were at peace."

There were other children on the estate, Leja knew, because she had once seen some children playing near the gatekeeper's house. But that was as close as she got to them for a long time. Her life consisted of learning and mischief and being dressed three times a day for meals. This latter was a tedious process for a young girl who only saw the same people for each meal and could see no reason for changing her clothes so often.

When she complained, her aunt would declare that there was something of the "plebian in you which refuses to live according to your station in life." The dress she often wore for the mid-day meal was a french blue dress, double pinch-pleated in the front and back. It was a lovely thing, but easily deranged if she didn't sit properly. The dress often cursed her day because three governesses, her French maid and the aunt would each remark, "You haven't sat correctly!" She soon came to hate the dress.

The only time of the day Leja was ever left alone was after the noon meal when the governesses and the aunt took a nap. Then she was allowed to go outside and walk in the park near the castle, keeping within carefully set bounds. One blue-dress day, she wandered farther than she was allowed to go. Suddenly she heard a noise that made her heart skip — the laughter of children. Running after the sound she found eight children playing behind an iron fence in the gatekeeper's garden. They were tossing a ball high in the air. Wonder of wonders, all at once the ball was at her feet and a small boy was saying, "Come and play with us"! What lovely words!

Leja squeezed through the fence, played and laughed and forgot time — until she heard shrill voices calling her name. She was found out, and worse, her blue dress was covered with mud and grass stains; she was disheveled and doubtless contaminated. Joy at finding her alive, and not kidnapped by gypsies, soon changed to anger. If she ever were so foolish again she would be locked up, given double homework, and whatever other awful punishments they could think of in the backwash of fear.

But she did do it again. And again. She wore her watch

and was careful to return in time to appear innocent. What excitement those days held! The children opened up a whole new world of fun and laughter to her. But eventually she was discovered and her punishment was as they had threatened — she was locked in her room. Leja cried herself ill, refusing food, people and books.

Once just after her mother's death Leja had tried to show her aunt affection, but had been sternly rebuked with words that hurt: "Hasn't your mother taught you better than to show emotion in public. A real lady never shows affection in front of others." Leja recalls, "My little heart froze." But the children, who had liked her, had called to her with excitement and joy each time she appeared, had brought a thaw. Now even this was taken away. Her starved heart was broken and life seemed useless.

The aunt suspected a naughty streak, yet the child's will to live seemed gone, so they called a physician.

The doctor knew nothing of the punishment, but after a brief examination and a quick evaluation of the household, he asked the right question: Did Leja have any friends her own age? No? In the interest of mental health, then, he advised that they send her away to school where she could be with other girls.

That was the answer, and Leja was promptly enrolled in an exclusive convent college in southern Germany to which daughters of royalty and nobility were sent. She was well-prepared by her three governesses for this advanced training, and practically beside herself with joy at being with a group. While her classmates crossed themselves for the days left until vacation came, Leja crossed herself for each day remaining until school began again.

Education at this college was not primarily religious because of the variety of backgrounds of students, but one nun, a professor of church history, did an unusual thing. She taught her class John 3:16 and made them recite it regularly. No matter how the class grumbled, she insisted that they repeat, "For God so loved the world, that he gave his only begotten Son, that whosoever believeth in him should not perish, but have everlasting life." Whatever else they may or may not have learned, the sister got that verse across.

At fifteen, with the equivalent of a university education behind her, Leja left school, returning to Latvia to marry the Baron de Torinoff, seventeen years her senior — a marriage arranged by the head of her family line. The baron was so handsome and dashing a man that his sophistication almost frightened Leja. As a second son the baron was propertyless, but as a member of the Russian nobility he was given command of a fortress at the edge of Siberia, controlling a large area of land for the Czar in a setting which gave him both power and adventure. There were no ladies' accommodations at the fortress, and Leja, now the baroness, lived in her castle in Latvia[1] hardly knowing the baron.

In the years that followed, the castle was often a place of lavish entertainment for royal heads of Europe. Kaiser Wilhelm danced with his hostess in the castle ballroom. Princes, dukes and earls from a dozen European countries were guests at various times of Baron and Baroness de Torinoff, for the baroness in her own right was the wealthiest woman in Latvia. Leja remembers that a solid gold dinner service was cached among other treasures in cabinets in the walls of the dining room. Such was the life of European nobility.

Leja was often troubled by the wretched poverty she observed not only in Riga, but in the large Russian cities. While the nobility lived luxuriously, the Russian peasantry practically starved. She spoke to her husband about the peasants who worked their own estate and asked if there wasn't some way to alleviate their illiteracy and squalor. But members of nobility were not interested in peasants, and smothered their fears of an uprising.

In 1914, World War I caught Russia poorly prepared for battle. As prewar tensions mounted, the German farm experts who managed the baroness' vast estate were called

---

[1]Latvia had been absorbed by Russia in the days of Peter the Great (ca. 1700). Its independent statehood between the two world wars was short-lived. Today it is a republic of the USSR.

home. And when war finally came, all the tenant farmers were conscripted into the armed forces, horses and wagons were requisitioned by the government, leaving fields of wheat unharvested as food became more and more scarce.

The Baron de Torinoff returned home for a brief visit and led his troops into East Prussia. His immediate success was soon reversed and the regiment was completely wiped out within a few days. Chaos and despair filled the country. Since the castle was close to the Prussian border, it was soon turned into a hospital by the Russian Red Cross. The baroness and other women of nobility volunteered as nurses. There were no medical supplies, and hardly any food to feed the dying soldiers. Hunger racked the bodies of the living, but sheer necessity drove them to go on living. The surgeon in charge of the castle was nearly eighty years old, and it seemed to the baroness that he always ran when called and never slept. Dying men were everywhere.

One day the baroness admitted bearers carrying a young boy, not yet sixteen. He had been wounded by the explosion of a shell, and both his skull and his lungs were exposed. From appearances he never should have lived to be brought this far. But he was alive and lying in the ballroom, a replica of the Hall of Mirrors in the Palace of Versaille — this peasant boy covered with bloody rags. The baroness felt delirious from fatigue and hunger, but knelt beside him to ask if there was a last message. "No last message, lady, but would you help me to pray?"

Leja panicked. She did not know how to pray. She looked frantically about for a priest. None was in sight. Only minutes were left for the boy, so she tried the Lord's prayer, but found she had forgotten it.

"It's too late," the boy moaned. "I'm lost. I'm lost." He repeated these words over and over.

Leja says now, remembering this incident, "I felt I was dying, too. Then suddenly as if my brain cells were being reactivated, I heard myself saying words I didn't recognize at first. I was saying the words of John 3:16. God was prompting me. The words came only one at a time."

Light came into the boy's face briefly as he listened, but then he moaned again, "It's too late. I'm lost."

Leja heard herself speak. She, who had scoffed and sneered when she had been taught this verse, was now saying, "Didn't you hear? Whosoever believeth in Him shall not perish, but have everlasting life. You must believe before it is too late."

As she pleaded with the boy to believe, her own heart was changed. Leja says, "He died believing in Jesus Christ. I lived believing. God came to me at that moment and revealed Himself."

A short time later the Germans swept into Latvia and took over her castle, and the baroness fled to St. Petersburg where she stayed with friends, doing what she could in the war effort.

Hard on the heels of the war came the Revolution, and Leja fled again, living in cellars to escape the mobs determined to exterminate the nobility. She was captured, impounded in the dungeon of the Peter and Paul Fortress in St. Petersburg, scheduled to be shot. "But God always put the right people near me," she comments, "and gave me faith in Himself." She was moved to another prison, then to a third, suffering exposure, privation and hunger such as she had never known. She clung to God and prayed for strength, for fortitude, for deliverance, and God answered. She finally managed to escape to Riga.

Only one of the fifty servants had remained at the castle. He was Peter, her faithful head steward, who had promised her mother that he would never desert Leja. Peter hid her, and for five months kept her out of sight, rising early to barter at the market for food to feed her. Eventually they set out together on foot, over muddy country roads for the harbor at the Gulf of Riga. No longer was there a Rolls Royce at her command. But they were picked up in a two-wheel cart along the way by the wife of a Swedish diplomat. She gave Leja the passport of her maid who had left her, and with God's help Leja was able to get passage on a steamer headed for Sweden.

Halfway up the gangplank when she was no longer on Russian soil, Peter, the faithful steward, gave her a small bag as his farewell to her. In it were some of the family jewels he had managed to salvage. They were Leja's worldly goods, and her passage to a new life.

Afraid of Europe in 1918, Leja went on to the United States and eventually got her papers straightened out. The new world offered a fresh beginning, and she helped earn her way by teaching German and French, and often gave thanks for the strict Miss Greene who had taught her English. At Tiffany's in New York she parted with some of the family pigeon-blood rubies to supplement her income. Having studied voice in Paris before the war, she now joined three paid choirs. No lack of opportunity in America.

Several years later, on one of these choir tours, an attractive widower named Charles Messenger escorted them on a tour of his city, Schenectady, New York. It was not difficult to fall in love with this warm-hearted Christian man, whom Leja married in 1926. Charles Messenger was God's special gift to this woman of a privileged class who had known so little of genuine love and godliness. Her husband helped teach her open, hungry mind the truth of the Bible. Leja says, "I was so spiritually starved I would have been open to any of the *isms* and cults, but God hedged me about until He could give me good teaching." The Messengers sat under the ministry of the First Presbyterian Church of Schenectady. At home they studied the Scriptures again, and Leja has come to love and know the Bible. Her words now at age seventy-six: "Do you wonder that I love this book?"

When Charles Messenger died in 1952, Leja Messenger began her third life. God had given her so much, she thought, she could give what was left of life for His service. She has a story to tell about God's love and faithfulness to boys and girls (her special love) and to men and women. Much younger than her years, she speaks as many as three times a week, and she *communicates* God's reality. She doesn't need to work this hard in one sense. She could relax and enjoy comfort and ease. She could say, "It's getting late. I must retire." But something compels her to drive a hundred miles on snowy nights over Michigan roads to talk about God and to spend weeks away from home traveling. She has never quite gotten used to the fact that God loved her enough to break into her life and reveal Himself when she needed Him most.

Sound like a fairy story? Leja Messenger says in the words of Jesus, "With men this is impossible; but with God all things are possible."[2]

---

[2]Matthew 19:26b.

5

Betty Carlson

Betty Carlson may well be one of your favorite writers, for she has eight published books, plus a weekly newspaper column called "I Love People." This is the story of how she came to have something important to say to the world.

THE ONLY ENTRY is on page one. Betty Carlson, age ten, wrote in her new diary:

> Dear Diary, It snowed yesterday, maybe we'll get snowed in and they'll have to close school. Cousin Eleanor gave me this diary for Christmas. Also I got skates, sox, 5 dollars, 3 books, boxing gloves and a flashlight. Guess I'll go to bed now I can read all night. P.S. Help me to learn to box good, God, so I can knock out them brothers of mine.

That was a short-lived writing career. But it was only the beginning. No one dreamed when she was ten that she would become a well-known writer who would make people laugh and reach up for higher ground. For it was not until many years and experiences later that she found she had something to say to the world.

Short-lived careers became a familiar routine to Betty Carlson. For instance, her career as a physical education teacher lasted all of three months. She tried to explain to the principal, who was speechless at her words, "I have decided to retire." Teachers retired after thirty years, not three months. But Betty told him that she already had a smothered sensation at the idea of daily going through the routine of picking up her clipboard, scooping up the volley balls and blowing her whistle at the students.

"When there are such marvelously exciting things to do in life," Betty said, "I can't bear the thought of spending my life blowing a whistle."

Her principal may never have recovered from the shock of her pronouncement. However, when he discovered that besides teaching she was taking flying lessons, playing in several orchestras, directing a scout troop, and enjoying a full social life, he marveled that she ever had found time to teach school in the first place.

When in doubt, go back to school. Many people before and since Betty have exercised this theory. It's a delicious retreat for restless people, and back to school Betty went.

A year later, she was ready to go to work again. If asked what she most wanted to do, she always shared her one big dream: to go to Switzerland. But Switzerland was out of the question in 1941, and so Betty took a job at the Women's Athletic Club in Chicago. She was hired to give private lessons in badminton, squash, diving and swimming. Squash was her prize accomplishment, but the women couldn't have cared less. Betty decided that most of the club's members were unaware that there even was a swimming pool or a squash court at the club. The only people who consistently used the facilities were Betty and the Swedish maid, Otillia, who was in charge of the locker room.

A year of this kind of life proved too dull and Betty again headed back to school. Only this time she went West! This time she was looking for more than the excitement of the university — she wanted to learn. She had lived long enough to collect some basic questions that she wanted answered. In fact, Betty was questioning everything these days. How could you know *that* was true? She would study and find out.

On an Oregon mountainside, Betty read Thomas Paine's *Age of Reason* and was appalled at her ignorance in blindly accepting what she had been taught in childhood. She had been blind, naive. Now she was liberated, she would believe what she wanted. And while only the mountain heard her say, "I choose not to believe," it wasn't long before this choice was increasingly evidenced in her life, as her staunch Lutheran background was thrown to the winds.

Questions beget questions. The more Betty asked, the more questions she found there were to ask, and the more restless and confused she became. In good Swedish tradition, she didn't bare her heart about this openly. In cowardice she pushed to the gloomy recesses of her consciousness any question she didn't like. But all was not misery. She worked at the U.S.O., she studied, she laughed and talked about life with budding intellectuals.

Walking through the post office to mail a letter one day, the "Join The Navy and See the World" poster caught her attention. It was the "seeing the world" bit that got to her. *Think I'll ask some questions about the* WAVES, Betty said to herself, and climbed the stairs to the recruiting office. She went in the door to ask questions, and came out of the door a WAVE.

"I never again came across that marvelous charm school hospitality I was met with in that recruiting office," Betty says amusingly — "not in any of my tours of duty which took me from New York to Hawaii. But those Navy years were a riotous, sobering and unforgettable experience."

After discharge, Betty Carlson was a veteran, and headed back to school to finish her Master's degree on the G.I. bill. The day she discovered that she could study in Europe on the G.I. bill, Betty rode on cloud nine. "Let's go survey the land," she said to her college roommate. Her roommate was agreeable — she wanted to take her mother to visit relatives in Norway. So Betty and her roommate cooked up a plan to tour Scandanavia and then join a youth hostel project in France which would include a bicycle trip through Switzerland. They left in the Spring, and it was a trip to be remembered.

When Betty returned home in the fall, she had one plan: to return to Europe as soon as possible. But thus far she had not proved very eloquently to her parents that she had serious intentions of ever working for a living. An attempt to impress them and herself with her great industry by working as a night maid in a large ocean-side hotel in Florida ended hilariously. Obviously she was meant to return to Europe.

This time she took her parents with her for a visit to Sweden, and made arrangements to stay on in Switzerland and study. The pension in Lausanne where she had reserved a room dampened the excitement of her adventure and its gloominess made her feel downright homesick. At least until she met Madame Dumreicher, a handsome, dignified German woman, one of the many unusual occupants of the pension. When no one at the door was able to understand what Betty hoped was French, Madame D. came to the rescue. "A little English I am speaking," she said, and became Betty's first friend in French-speaking Lausanne.

"I am not with the ears hearing too well," Madame Dumreicher would say, pulling out a long, curved ear trumpet from her bag. Placing it to her ear, she would direct Betty to speak into it. But their friendship was sealed when she learned Betty had bicycled from Sweden. Madame Dumreicher grabbed Betty and hugged her, laughing and exclaiming in her deep voice, "You Americanes are all quite wonderfully mad." From then on she took Betty under her wing and did away with the Madamoiselle Carlson routine. "I shall call you Bettily," she said.

This grand old German friend did much to make Betty's first year in Switzerland. Baroness Maria von Dumreicher had one of the riches to rags stories so familiar to those of noble birth in Europe. She and Betty spent hours drinking tea from chipped cups, in their dingy rooms with streaked, faded wallpaper. But somehow with Madame D. there even that atmosphere had elegance. For six months these two lived together in the dark pension with its peculiar residents. Then openings came and each moved to pleasanter quarters. But Madame D.'s friendship with Betty was a God-arranged affair, as you'll see later.

Betty was enrolled at the Music Conservatory in Lausanne, and it was there that Bernie and Charlie, two American students, came into her life. They introduced her to Madame Robert and her family with whom Betty came to live. Madame Robert's missionary husband had been killed in Madagascar, and she was now raising their three children by giving piano lessons and renting out rooms. It was a delightful family, and Bernie and Charlie were among the boarders. Everyone in the house loved music, and although the noise was deafening at times, it was an exciting place to live. Certainly it was not gloomy and quiet like the first pension.

Coffee hour with Madame Robert was the highlight of the day. After dinner, the family went to the living room for coffee, conversation, music and relaxation. This was home. One evening Madame Robert told the group that her seventeen-year-old son, Jean Paul, was coming home for the holidays. She explained that he was not well; in fact, he was gravely ill. She hoped he and Betty would become friends.

From the beginning Jean Paul and Betty Carlson seemed to understand each other. Jean Paul was sensitive, alert, and very well-read. They would sit together on the balcony in the sunshine, overlooking the mountains and the blue lake below, wrapped in coats and blankets, and talk about life, about books, about their families. One day he told her about his illness, that he had cancer. Then he asked, "Betty, do you ever think about death?"

It was unfair to tell her this and ask the question at the same time. Betty asked lots of questions, but death was one she always covered over. So he had hit her most sensitive point on both counts. That great, gnawing dark fear ate at her insides, but she seldom let it come to the surface. Now she quickly changed the subject.

But Jean Paul would not let it go so easily. He explained softly, "Betty, you must not fear to think of death, for it can be almost a friend."

Those words came back to haunt Betty Carlson when she heard of Jean Paul's death the next summer. She and Bernie had spent hours on the balcony discussing the philosophers, and enjoying for a brief season the puffed up sense of well-being that comes with much talk. They almost concluded that they were clever and wise. But they had never faced death.

After Jean Paul's death, Madame Dumreicher wrote that in all his suffering Jean Paul sat, "holding his Bible with a strong faith in his heart. Schatzi," she said, "he was so stalwart a Christian." It was over Jean Paul that Betty prayed the first sincere prayer she had prayed since she was little. "Why, God, did you take his life and leave behind one like me?" Was this peace an exclusive possession of Jean Paul?

Meanwhile Betty made some progress in her career search. She decided she wanted to be a writer. It was a glorious idea, but when she started asking *Who am I? What have I got to say?* she found she was stuck. Through Madame D. she met Carol, an American student studying psychology. Carol said that all her writer friends were undergoing psychoanalysis, "because how can you write if you don't understand yourself?" Betty agreed on that point and arranged to see a qualified analyst in Lausanne. No startingly new discoveries were made during her twice-weekly visits to the analyst. Both the analyst and Betty concluded there was a desperate inner emptiness in her life, but neither had any suggestions of how it could be filled.

Betty went home for summer vacation full of descriptions of the glories of Switzerland. She worked at Camp Eleanor on Lake Geneva, Wisconsin, that summer as a swimming and tennis instructor. There she talked Gea, the music instructor, into exploring the majesty of Switzerland with her.

Betty was a pretty good saleswoman, because Gea didn't like traveling and hesitated leaving her boyfriend unattached for a year. But Betty's description of the great piano, drama, and ballet teachers available in Lausanne was too much for Gea to resist and she agreed to go. Betty also talked her father into *one more year of Switzerland* for her career's sake.

During their first month in Lausanne it rained every day, and their room in a damp, cheap boardinghouse was so cold their words hung in the air. Gea was not hesitant to let Betty know twenty or thirty times a day that she wished she had never come, and Betty returned the compliment. When they heard through a friend about another apartment, described as the most over-heated apartment in Lausanne, they snapped it up even though it was seventy-five steps up to the fifth floor. It even had a fireplace to add to its warmth, and the girls declared it charming.

The overheated apartment was just right for two American girls used to central heating. There they thawed out to appreciate the marvels of Lausanne. First Gea worked hard on her piano lessons. Until that enthusiasm waned. Then she took ballet lessons, and "the dance" became her life. She would leap into the kitchen with a *grand jeté,* pirouette out of the door, and generally make life a little breathless.

One evening she decided that Betty, too, must become enamored with "the dance." Betty must wear one of her "tu-tus," she grandly insisted, and come with her for a ballet lesson and meet the "Maitre de Dance." Betty succumbed and let Gea put her into a yellow tu-tu (which stuck out hopelessly in the rear), and long black stockings and ballet slippers. Even Betty's waddling around the room uttering appropriate "quack-quacks" did not put off the zealous Gea. She was out to transform this athletic, well-built woman into a ballerina.

It can honestly be said that the class, Gea, the Maitre de Dance, and even Betty, all tried hard to make her a success. The air was filled with music and gleeful dancers. Things were going fairly well until it was time for the great leap — the *grand jeté*. That did it! Gea's yellow tu-tu, too small for Betty, couldn't take the strain and split right down the middle. Thus the ballerina career ended. Neither of them mentioned it again, and shortly thereafter even Gea tired of "the dance."

The two girls were dismayed at how often they were tired of life in general. Gea enrolled in an art class at the university for a new interest. Betty worked on the musical end of her career, but often she found herself in black, ornery moods over nothing. One night after she had quarreled with Gea over the foul temper she had displayed, Betty went out for a long, brisk walk, wanting to get away from Gea, away from herself. She walked hard and fast, as if she were being pursued. When she came to a park, she slumped over on her favorite bench, and watched the moon make its path on Lake Geneva. She tried to ignore it, but a Presence was there.

She whispered, "God?"

And then as she spoke His name, her despair poured out and she wept over the details of her life. She hadn't cried that hard since she was a child.

Back in the apartment Betty broached the subject of religion with Gea and they talked far into the night about what they might be missing by not having a religious faith. The *Lausanne Gazette* carried an announcement of Bible lectures at the university, and they decided to go. The professor's liberal approach to the Scriptures finished them. It was clear that he had nothing positive to offer from either the Scriptures or his own life. As they had suspected, the Bible was unreliable, and they put it back on the shelf. Soon they got caught up in a new whirl of interests and were too busy to worry about their quest for purpose.

But you do have to have a cause to live for, and Betty went on a "good-will-among-men" binge. She was enthusiastic over the idea of a United States of Europe, and began writing articles urging American students to come to Europe and study. She mailed her manuscripts back home, and the *Miami Herald* published one of them.

The article was read by a young sailor who wrote to her via the *Miami Herald*. Betty was secretly encouraged by her fan mail, even though the sailor pointed out a severe omission in her good-will message. "There is no good will apart from Christ," the sailor said, and backed up his statements with a string of Bible verses.

Bible quoters made Betty furious, especially if they were trying to prove she was wrong. She wrote back a cheerfully scathing letter along the lines of "welcome to the twentieth century," and suggested that he get a few books and do a little up-to-date reading.

The sailor replied, very kindly, but firmly, that Betty Carlson was the one who was wrong and suggested she read the Bible.

She returned an answer designed to finish the sailor-boy off for good, but he didn't finish that easily. His letters were firm, intelligent and confident. And full of Bible verses. He corresponded so regularly that Gea and Betty began to look forward to the missive, and declared he must not be doing much for the Navy since he had so much time to write. He sent more than letters — magazines, booklets, tracts and articles, book markers with Bible verses began to arrive in a deluge.

Gea would ask, "What has your sailor friend sent today?" when the mailman came. And there would almost always be something. Betty could never resist the printed page and looked it over more carefully than she sometimes wished she had.

Life, which had been moving along somewhat drearily, suddenly picked up in tempo. All kinds of things happened. First of all, Betty and Gea got the idea of taking a good-will tour through Europe on a motor scooter, so they went out and bought one. Gea bought a lute; Betty bought a mandolin. They would hit the road when summer came, like motor-scooter troubadours. But they needed a third party for the act, so they wrote to their Camp Eleanor friend, Marianne, who had all kinds of musical talent.

Marianne agreed to come, only when she arrived, she wasn't the same Marianne. Gea and Betty were sure she had flipped. She came with a Bible which she read every night, and kept trying to tell them about something wonderful that had happened to her. Almost as bad as the sailor. Also, to top it all off, she didn't like the musical good-will idea once she understood what it was about.

Trouble didn't end there. Betty was hospitalized with a sinus infection and, as she describes it, was operated on in a foreign language. Gea and Marianne ruined the motor scooter by ramming it into a taxi cab. Thus ended good will for everyone concerned. Marianne went off to see the rest of Europe before returning to the States. A friend suggested that Betty and Gea go to the mountains for a holiday to recover from their troubles. It was a good idea, but the mandolin, the lute and the motor scooter had left their resources sadly depleted.

Mail call the next day brought a letter from dear Madame Dumreicher, who was now living with her nephews in England. A year or so earlier, when they were in Lausanne together, Madame D. had been very excited about a family she had visited in Champery. She wanted Betty to visit them, too. "I cannot explain," she had said, "but this people is going to be of magnitude to you some day. You must be meeting them." These were details Betty had long since forgotten.

Now she tore open the letter and read:

> I am just receiving a letter from the Schaeffers in Champery. They are demanding me, dear, if you are still in Switzerland and why you are no visiting them. I only ask you, Schatzi, why are not?

Betty whooped out Gea's name, and read her the letter. "We're going to the mountains!" she said, and Gea responded with a few *grand jetés* of joy. Betty sat down and wrote to the Schaeffers, and almost immediately received a letter welcoming them.

Gea packed enough luggage to last a year. (The taxi driver said, "Have a nice summer," and they were too embarrassed to tell him they were only going for a week or two!) Champery is a well-known resort area and Gea pictured herself at romantic dinners, whirling around the dance floor with a new date every evening. Betty argued all the way about the twelve pairs of shoes Gea insisted on taking, but she, too, was looking forward to a gay time.

This was the girls' first visit into the mountain villages of Switzerland, and they were enchanted. This was the *real* Switzerland! Music-box chalets with window boxes filled with geraniums hung like ornaments on the mountainside. Church spires, covered bridges, quaint villages, valleys, shining mountain peaks — it was unbelievable. Finally the end of the line up the mountainside was Champery.

At the railway station Gea and Betty were met by the Schaeffers' young daughter Debbie and by Marlise, one of the older helpers at the chalet, pulling a small wagon as transport for the girls' luggage. Debbie's eyes grew wide when she saw the immense pile to be carried to the chalet. Betty came to the rescue by insisting that they leave her bag of books and golf clubs at the station for a later pickup. The four began to walk across the village to the Schaeffer's chalet.

Champery is the kind of town the picture books show as Switzerland. It was everything Betty Carlson had been looking for right down to the Swiss cows with the huge bells around their necks, and the scampering goats straight from *Heidi*. It was a long walk (Debbie and Marlise took turns pulling the heavy wagon), and the setting sun turned the peaks to a flaming red as evening came to this charming town. Walking beside Debbie, Betty was in ecstasy.

Although Debbie was only a child, she talked like a grown-up, as she explained the village, the valley and the fact that her parents had been called away and would return soon. When Betty spoke of the marvel of the scenery, this child stirred her own childhood memories by remarking, "It makes me wonder what heaven will be like. The Bible says we haven't seen anything yet."

Later upstairs in their room at the Schaeffer's chalet, Gea turned on Betty as soon as they were alone.

"Schatzi, ole dear," she said, "you have just gotten us into the tightest spot of our lives. These people are *missionaries*!

You were so busy looking at the mountains and the cows, you didn't even hear what Marlise told me. You and your precious Madame Dumreicher have gotten us in with a bunch of missionaries." Betty struggled to get the picture, while Gea swore. *What had Madame D. said about these wonderful stimulating friends in the mountains? Missionaries . . .?* Good grief, this was too much!

It was true. The Schaeffers *were* missionaries. The kind that started all their meals with long prayers, the kind who talked about spiritual matters in every conversation, and always quoted the Bible. The very worst kind, Betty thought. After dinner, Mr. Schaeffer conducted a Bible study and prayed some more. Besides this, the family was always gathering around the piano and singing hymns. Gea and Betty thought it a colossal performance on their behalf, and it made them very uncomfortable, to say the least. They tried to beg off, to disappear, but it was such a part of their daily routine that they couldn't escape all of it.

Betty and Gea slept in on purpose each morning, and Debbie served them breakfast on the large, lower balcony overlooking the beautiful valley. Debbie or Priscilla or Susan the Schaeffers' daughters — always stopped to talk, and it was from them the girls found out that the family came from St. Louis and Mr. Schaeffer taught Bible classes.

As the days passed by, the girls could not long resist the charm and hospitality of their hosts. They went into Champery to look up a Lausanne friend, Angela, who worked in a hotel there. When Angela found out where they were staying she made a remark about the Schaeffers being fanatical about their religion. To their surprise, Betty and Gea found themselves rushing to the Schaeffers' defense. Quite heatedly they told Angela that they were the nicest family they had ever met.

The cordial Schaeffers invited Angela to dinner one evening. Edith Schaeffer had a way with meals. Not only was the food delicious, but it was cooked with love! Love pervaded the whole chalet. *That's what makes it so special,* thought Betty. And on this particular night she had added an extra touch

— baking powder biscuits for Gea, who hadn't had them since she left America.

Dinner conversation turned to the subject of peace, and one of the Schaeffer children commented that real peace comes when people believe in God. Mrs. Schaeffer added that most people choose not to believe in God or in the Bible, God's Word, and how there can be no peace unless there is an ultimate truth.

This was too much for Angela. She spoke with feeling. She had always believed all religions were equally good, that all roads lead to God, that Christianity cannot claim to be the only truth.

Listening to all these conversations, Betty was beginning to get the picture. "Excuse me, Angela," she interrupted, "but for the first time things are making sense to me. If we say all religions are equally good, we make God kind of a benevolent floor walker in a department store. It really belittles God and makes Him look terribly foolish and disorganized." She went on to explain that she had always thought as Angela did, that this was the only intelligent way to explain other people's good intentions in their religions. Suddenly she saw how stupid it was. Why, even a foreman in a small factory was better organized than this vague god-of-anything-goes which she had believed in.

No one was more surprised than she was to hear herself say these things. Stunned, the group around the table went on listening and she went on talking.

"If God made me, and I believe He did, it doesn't make sense that He would just throw me out into the world and not bother ever to communicate with me — like maybe in a book or through a person. It seems silly that He would have several people all saying different things."

Then Betty went on to say that she thought when she returned to the States that she would take a whirl at Hebrew and Greek at this seminary Mr. Schaeffer had mentioned and see for herself if the Bible is God's message to men.

Silence. Then Gea spoke and said she wasn't interested in

any old seminary; she was interested in a deep peace inside of her right now.

Edith Schaeffer was quick to explain that one didn't get that peace through knowing Hebrew or Greek, but by knowing Jesus Christ, the source of all peace. Angela interrupted her, somewhat bitterly, "You can never make me believe that!"

To which Mr. Schaeffer replied that Angela was absolutely right. Only the Spirit of God can open eyes and help people to see and believe the truth. Then he told his own story, of his disillusionment, of his finally meeting God in the person of Jesus Christ.

When Gea objected to the idea that God might make her a missionary with clumsy shoes and a bun on the back of her head, Mrs. Schaeffer said something both girls would never forget. "Gea we're talking about the infinite God who has infinite imagination. I'm sure that if you do accept the Lord, He will have a wonderful plan for your life, something special, something right for you."

Later Betty and Gea walked Angela back to her hotel, and returned to the chalet to pack. They were going home the next day. The days had passed too quickly.

The suitcases packed and in the hallway the next day, Betty sought out Edith Schaeffer, who was changing sheets in one of the bedrooms. "You know, Edith," she said, "I'm reconsidering what we talked about last night. I told you I planned to spend the summer reading the Bible, and then make a decision about whether or not I think it is truth. Well, I've been thinking and I've come to another conclusion. You said that when one accepts Jesus Christ, then the Holy Spirit comes to live in that person and makes the Bible clear. Well, it seems foolish to me to study the Bible without all the help I can get. . . . I think I'll accept Christ right now and then have His help all summer before going to seminary."

Edith Schaeffer dropped the pillow she was changing and rushed over to hug Betty. Then together they prayed that God would accept Betty as His child, not because she deserved it, but because Christ had died on the cross on her behalf. That's how Betty Carlson became a member of God's family, a Christian.

Downstairs Gea was writing her name in the guest book. The Schaeffers didn't discover what she had written until after they had put the girls on the train to Lausanne. Then they read,

> Little did I know that in coming to Chalet Bijou, I would finally find the Christ I've been looking for so many years. My gratitude to you for showing me the way.

There in the Swiss mountains Gea scribbled out her confession of faith and Betty Carlson bowed her proud head in an upstairs bedroom, and both entered into Life.

Later that summer they visited Madame Dumreicher in England, and laughed and cried a little while recounting their visit to Champery. Betty asked, "Why didn't you tell me they were missionaries?"

Madame D. smiled sweetly and winked at Gea, "Oh, didn't I tell you?" she said.

Today Gea is married to a minister, has eight children and two dogs, and in moments of joy she still can make a *grand jeté*. Life as a parson's wife isn't always easy, but Gea knows the deep peace and joy she talked about that night at dinner in Champery.

But this is Betty's story, and you'll want to know what has happened to her. She did go to seminary. The more she learned, the more she found out there was to learn. She decided that discovering all there was to know about God was a lifetime job. She began to see what it meant to live in fellowship with Jesus Christ, and it was the biggest challenge she has ever known. Life made sense, and she found out she had something to say about it. Betty has become a writer as she one day hoped she would.

In the Middle West, people know Betty Carlson for her weekly column in *The Rockford Morning Star* called, "I Love People," which appears also in Iowa, Missouri and Wisconsin newspapers.

Her books — eight of them at this writing — are like warm

conversations with a woman who finds it exciting to know God. Her style is fresh and realistic. She says to people, "This is what I am learning. . . ," and because it comes out of her own life, her readers catch the significance of what she says for their own lives.

And you can't imagine what else God has done for this lover of Switzerland. He has given her a chalet. Betty calls her purchase of this chalet "God-covered recklessness," and says this is one of the delightful things she has learned about God. He does have infinite imagination — and infinite love.

Sometime after the Schaeffers moved to another village in Switzerland, they wrote to tell her of a beautiful chalet for sale situated just below theirs on the mountainside just outside of Huemoz. Betty bought it sight unseen and called it Chalet Le Chesalet. Whether she is there or not, the house is used as an overflow for L'Abri guests who come to the Swiss Alps to find out if God is relevant in this age.

It's a beautiful place. I know, because we were at Chalet Le Chesalet ourselves as guests. I sat on Betty's balcony and overlooked the magnificent valley in springtime — saw the mountain peaks and the wild flowers and was led to tell God how much I loved Him. It's that kind of a place.

Betty smiles over her career-less past and says there is nothing like the monthly payments of a chalet to encourage one to work and settle on a career. The real stability, however, has come from having that inner emptiness filled. She looked for a long time and had many adventures, but none was exhilarating and satisfying as knowing the triune God of the universe.

6

Leah Marshel

The synagogue was familiar to Leah Marshel, but God seemed harsh, vindictive towards her people, and far away. Then one day as a teenager she heard that God loved her — *so much that He had sent Jesus Christ to die for her. That message changed her life. Today Leah Marshel is a missionary in Latin America, sharing that same message with others.*

THE MERCY OF THE LORD. I had heard that phrase from the Psalms many times in the synagogue, only it was in the Hebrew language and not at all related to my life. Today God's mercy fills me with awe, for He reached down into a Jewish family and revealed Himself to me in the Person of Jesus Christ. I knew I had met *Him,* and I began to know what mercy was.

My parents were living in Georgia along the Black Sea when the Russian Revolution broke out in 1917. I really don't know many of the details, except that they were wealthy and had to leave behind all their possessions when they escaped to safety. Eventually they arrived in Germany and my father started from the bottom to earn a living. He began by selling handkerchiefs and hosiery, and as time went on he managed to set up quite a business for himself. Once more my parents became very prosperous.

While they were in Germany my oldest brother Gabriel and two of my sisters, Sarah and Esther, were born. My parents were orthodox Jews, and when the Nazis came into power and Jewish persecution began in Germany, my father was thrown into prison. He suffered many hardships and was made to do slave labor. Again I don't know many of the details, but in some way my mother was able to get him out of prison and they escaped with their family to London, England. For the second time all their possessions were left behind.

It is not surprising that these two experiences scarred the lives of my parents. They were bitter about the world, and their main ambition in London was to make money. Even as a child I knew this was the goal in life. Father began from "scratch" again, this time as a manufacturer of underwear, and the business prospered. Two other children were born, Simha and Raphael, and then I came along into the world. Later another sister was born, Elizabeth.

By then our family was doing well. As a young child I can recall having a governess. Our family language was German and the governess taught me English. We also had a housekeeper. But for some reason that I will never know until I get to heaven, my parents seemed to favor Gabriel, Sarah and Simha more than Raphael, Esther or myself. The older ones received better treatment and many more material things than we did.

I only learned Esther's story much later. She was so ill-treated and beaten that she ran away from home when she was eleven years old. Later Raphael and I were very cruelly dealt with in our home. It seems so strange that in a household with seven children, three should be favored and the rest treated as though they did not belong. In fact, we were told in no uncertain terms that we did not fit into the family. Raphael and I were looked on at the level of the maid. We were beaten often, and seemingly without reason. I do not know why this happened. All I know is that I grew up as a very miserable young child. I hated my home and everything about it. I remember walking up and down the streets wondering how my life would turn out.

I had gone to a Jewish boarding school for a time and received training in Hebrew and religious instruction from the Old Testament. We didn't understand much of what was being said at the synagogue, and besides, the women and children seemed remotely removed since they had to sit upstairs. As far as God was concerned, I didn't think much of Him. I just remember my parents saying that it was important to go to the synagogue because it would help them prosper. God wouldn't let them down if they kept the sabbath and other Jewish traditions.

There were so many inconsistencies in our home. Everything in the kitchen was kept kosher. We kept meat and milk separate. We kept the sabbath. No one was allowed to turn on a light, cook anything or even hold money in their pocket on the sabbath. But we had a maid and if she did all these things for us it was all right. I thought religion was a lot of trashy tradition. God was just someone who was punishing me and I couldn't figure out what I was doing wrong. God and my parents seemed equally unkind. I was growing up in deadly fear of my mother, and so was Raphael.

I didn't understand until much later that the housekeeper who came to our house when I was ten years old was a born-again Christian. Her husband was in the war and she worked for us during that time. When my mother wanted to get rid of me for a while, she often sent me to the housekeeper's house. This was supposed to be a kind of punishment, but I loved going there because I was treated so well.

On one occasion my parents went to the United States to establish business contacts there, so they sent me to stay with the housekeeper for a few weeks. While I was there, a young woman came to the house. She seemed all excited and told our housekeeper that she had accepted Jesus Christ as her Saviour. The housekeeper tried to shush her up a bit, trying to indicate that I was a Jew. When she understood from the conversation that I was Jewish, she only talked to me more about Jesus Christ.

I was dumbfounded. The only way I had ever heard about Jesus Christ was in blasphemy. As far as His being a Saviour, I had never heard of such a thing! I had no qualms about telling her that I thought she was a crazy fanatic, and not to talk to me about him because I didn't believe in him. As far as I was concerned he was the scum of the earth. At fifteen and a half that is as much as I knew, but I sounded off like I thought a Jewess should.

My wild words didn't scare her off. She just kept on loving me. She often asked me to go for a walk and I would go, thinking I'd just tell her off some more if she brought up the subject again. But her kindness disarmed me. One night she asked me to go to a meeting with her. She said the speaker would talk about Jesus Christ, and after all Jesus Christ was a Jew, so why didn't I come and hear about Him. I was afraid and said no.

That night I couldn't sleep, and I thought about the meetings. I was curious. I decided I would go and then I would make such a noise and disturbance that she would be sorry she ever invited me. So I went with her the next night to an evangelistic service held in Westminister Central Hall in London. To my horror two or three thousand people were there singing hymns. Then a bishop got up and talked about the Lord Jesus Christ. He said Christ loved me so much that He was willing to die on the cross to pay the penalty for my sins.

I'll never forget those words. They went deeply into my starved heart. I don't remember much of what else was said that night. I just recall going home literally stunned by what I had heard. In bed that night the bitterness over years of not feeling loved broke, and I cried as I had never cried before. Something about Christ's love made all the ugliness of my life seem so awful. All the hatred I felt toward my parents for their cruelty seemed so wretched. My pillow was wet with tears, and I felt an intense longing for whatever my life needed to make me feel satisfied, to give me peace. I wanted Someone who would love me and care about my life. I felt so desperately alone that night.

The next morning my friend who had taken me to the meeting called on the phone. Suddenly I was asking her how I could become a Christian. It was a completely strange thing for me to say and I had never heard those words used quite that way before. Why I said them, I don't know; I believe God put them in my mouth. My friend said, "Leah, you go back to your room and simply ask Jesus Christ to come into your life."

Back in my room, I knelt down by my bed because I had heard that Christians kneel, but I didn't quite understand what my friend had said. "Oh God," I prayed, "tell me what she is talking about and I'll do it." I got up from the bed, overwhelmed at what was happening to me, and went downstairs where I saw a Bible lying on the table. I opened it to the New Testament because again I had heard Christians use the New Testament. My eyes fell on John 3:16. It was just the verse I needed. God loved me so much . . . that He gave His son . . . and He wanted me to believe in Him.

I kept mulling that verse over in my mind. When my friend came by that evening I said to her, "Is this an important verse?" and showed her the Bible.

"Oh, Leah," she said, "this is the key to the whole Scripture." She explained it to me again, and then told me that God was calling me to Himself. She told me that if I hadn't understood before to return to my room and make sure I asked Jesus Christ to come into my life. I did. And He received me into God's family.

I had about a week in the housekeeper's home in which to learn all I could about Jesus Christ. The meeting I had attended was one of a series of evangelistic meetings being held in 1951 to celebrate the festival of Britain year. Tom Rees was the evangelist, and I went every night. I was thrilled to learn the Christian hymns and choruses. One chorus I remembered especially and it stood by me in the ensuing weeks.

Jesus Christ is the Way,
Jesus Christ is the Truth,
Jesus Christ is the Life,
And He's mine, mine, mine.

I can't know today how many times I sang that over and over in my mind after the real difficulties came.

One night when I was at the meeting about a week after I became a Christian, the loudspeaker called, "Would Miss Leah Marshel go to the front lobby, please?" I knew it was a message saying that my parents had returned home. As I was leaving the meeting, the congregation was singing,

There is a green hill far away
Without a city wall,
Where the dear Lord was crucified
Who died to save us all,
Oh dearly, dearly has he loved
And we must love Him, too,
And trust in His redeeming blood
And try His works to do.

It's strange the things one remembers. I was only fifteen and a half, but those words were like God's message to me.

On the train returning home, I wondered how I could tell my parents what I had done, but I couldn't think of any way. Fear and trembling were real emotions to me because I truly feared my parents. Disobedience was unknown in our house. How did you tell Jewish parents that you had become a Christian? That was worse than saying you had become a Gentile.

The next day I conceived a plan — a foolish one born in the heart of a confused teenager. I decided that if I could make my mother very angry, then I would have her attention and she would get out a stick and beat me. Then in the tenseness of the moment I could tell her that I was a Christian. So I got the teapot full of tea and in front of my mother I spilled it all over the tablecloth. I got her attention sure enough. When her anger subsided I said, "Mother, I just have to tell you something. I can't concentrate this morning. I have become a Christian."

My mother went pale and she was speechless for a moment. "What do you mean, you've become a Christian?" she asked.

"I've accepted Jesus Christ into my heart," I said.

"Well, you can't do that," she answered finally, "You are not twenty-one yet. No girl can make a decision like that until after she is twenty-one."

I said, "Mother, this just happened. It's in my heart."

"Wait until your father comes home and we'll see about whether it is in your heart or not!"

Later that evening the whole family gathered around the table as a council of examination. The household was in a dither, everyone was shocked and questioned me at length. My older brother Gabriel was a Cambridge graduate and supposedly very clever. He said, "Leah, how could Jesus Christ be born of a virgin. Mary was just a prostitute."

"I don't know what you mean," I said, "but I do know He is in my heart."

They continued to question me and spoke contemptuously to me. A Christian is simply filth in a Jewish household. They gave me three weeks to change my mind. If I did not, then I would have to go.

My parents were sending me to a fashionable finishing school at this time. At eighteen the girls in my school would become debutantes and be presented to Her Majesty the Queen. It really doesn't fit together — that I should be sent to that kind of a school and be so poorly treated at home at the same time. But that is the way it was.

During the next week I tried to contact my friend. I wrote letters to her while doing my homework, telling her how much I loved the Lord. I read my Bible secretly. One night my mother gave me money for a movie and I went to the Tom Rees meetings instead. Another time I wanted to go so badly and the only way I could devise was to sneak out across the narrow window ledge of our apartment house to the fire escape on the other side of the building. It was a narrow squeak and my heart was in my throat the whole way. When I reached the fire escape I found I had my slippers on, so I had to go all the way back for my shoes and then inch my way across that narrow ledge another time. My friends were shocked to see me at the meetings and afraid of what might happen to me.

The next morning I got a beating for being out of the house. From then on my activities were watched very closely and I was not given many privileges. About two and a half weeks after I had come home from the housekeeper's house, my mother found a Bible hidden in my handbag. With it was a letter I had written my friend containing much about Christianity and also about my family and the way they were treating me. Mother tore the Bible into shreds, and then got a stick and beat me unmercifully. She pulled my hair out in chunks, dragged me across the floor, hit me with a shoe, then with the stick again. All in all, she did a thorough job.

When I staggered to my feet at last, hurting all over, my mother said, "This is it. Either you give up this Jesus Christ or you get out."

"Mother, how can I give up Jesus Christ when He is in my heart? I just cannot do that," I said.

She said, "That's it, then."

I got my coat. I had on only old clothes, play clothes, if you like. I wondered where I would go and what I would do as I walked out of the door. My mother stood at the door shouting, "Leah, you're going to regret this. You're going to regret this until the end of your days."

Never was a child more confused or scared. The pain from the beating numbed my mind, but I did have three pennies in my pocket. In England that is enough to make a phone call, so I called the housekeeper. I remembered, too, the Scripture I had read, "When my mother and my father forsake me, then the Lord will take me up."[1] He certainly did that.

---

[1]Psalm 27:10.

Mother called the police and told them I had run away from home and that she wanted me back. My friends also contacted the police because I was a minor. The police came to the housekeeper's house and could see in one look that I had been badly beaten. They went back to my mother and asked her to explain why I had been so mistreated. My mother said I had been disobedient and that she really wanted me back. After a few days of discussion back and forth, the police made the stipulation that if my mother wanted me she would come and get me.

One Sunday night as I was returning from church I saw my mother come out of the house where I was staying. She had a policeman with her, and a taxi waiting in front. I stayed away from the house until they left. From that day on she never tried to get me back. I only saw my mother once after that, about six months later when I called her to ask if I could be baptized. She was very angry and impatient with me. That was the last time I ever saw her. (She died in 1954.) If I had gone home I don't know what would have happened to me. I do know life would have been misery, and perhaps I might not even be alive today. I believe God protected my life at this time.

The adjustment to my new life was not easy. Of course I could not expect my parents to pay the bill for me at the expensive school. At fifteen and a half in England it is possible for a girl to go to work, but I was poorly trained for that kind of life. I had no experience in even the simplest things. The only clothes I now owned were the ones I had on.

My friend took me to the pastor of her church and God's family there shared my problem. I remember how thrilled I was when, after we had prayed, a telephone call came with the offer of a new dress. Within a few days I had a new wardrobe. The pastor and the people got together and sent me to a secretarial school where I learned shorthand and typing. I lived with the housekeeper and I had never been so loved and cared for in my life. And Jesus Christ was in my heart.

At eighteen I went into the nursing profession. I was then old enough to realize that God had His hand upon me in an unusual way. I wanted to serve Him and so I went into nursing with that in mind. In England nurses are paid to train, so it was a simple matter to work my way through school.

During my first year of nursing, the Moody Chorale came to London. I was thrilled by their concert, their conduct and their personal words. I began to pray that I might come to the United States to study at Moody Bible Institute. Years later, in 1959, I did come to study at Moody. I had worked for nine months as a staff nurse in the operating room and had made sufficient money for a trip to America. The Cheam Baptist Church of Surrey, England, gave me a gift to cover my first term at Moody. Nursing in Chicago provided the rest of the funds.

These years were not easy ones. Having left home so young, with so little guidance and security in my early life, I faced many difficulties. Sometimes I felt the struggles would drown me. I had times of great despondency. My ups and downs must have been hard on the people closest to me. But God, the great problem-solver, just kept hanging onto me and brought me through.

My mother had told me so often how ugly I was and how ashamed she was of me that I found it hard to believe anyone could love me, least of all God. I struggled with this problem for years. My insecurity urged me to do all the wrong things on purpose to get attention. At Moody I often acted the role of a rebel to get others concerned. All the while God and His family kept on loving me and helping me to accept myself so that I could begin to be free to think of others. When I took psychology at Michigan State University a few years later, I began to understand myself in a new way.

As I came to understand myself as an adult, I also came to know God better and my life was stabilized. While I was studying at Michigan State I worked as a counselor in one of the dormitories, and God opened my eyes to see the needs of others. I realized how miserable many students were, torn by the philosophies of this world. Their lives seemed confused, bewildered and often full of sham. I knew I had found the answer to some of these same needs in Jesus Christ and that He would do this for these students, too. I asked God, if it were His will, to send me to work somewhere among university students.

I felt increasingly certain God wanted me on the foreign mission field and so I applied to a missionary society. While I was at candidate school I learned the mission was looking for workers among the university students in Venezuela. As soon as I finish language school in Costa Rica, I plan to go to Maracaibo to work among students, sharing what I have learned about Jesus Christ.

Occasionally I see my family. Each year my father invites me to spend a weekend in New York with him. He takes me to the top hotels and the best nightclubs in an effort to show me what I am missing. Simha keeps trying to bring the whole family back together and is more sympathetic towards me than some of the others, although she says she is ashamed of what I am doing. My father keeps reminding me of all the money I am not making, while the others have varying opinions about my sanity.

And I keep praying for a miracle which will introduce them all to the wonder of knowing Jesus Christ, who gives Life.

7
Jane Stuart Smith

Jane Stuart Smith's dream in life was to be an opera star, a prima donna. That, *she thought,* would make me completely happy. *Her dream came true and she won the applause of opera audiences across Europe. But it wasn't enough; something was missing.*

JANE STUART SMITH has more exciting memories than most of us. At least hers are more like the stuff out of which story books and dreams are made. The applause of the opera world for a prima donna, the thrill of a superb performance, the satisfaction of success, these are things Jane Smith knows about. The press awaited her arrival at the airports of the world, and her home town turned out to say they loved her. She knew the magic of capturing a role and holding the emotions of the audience in her hands. She has been the Princess Turandot, Norma and Brunnhilde, and those who saw and heard her were pleased, and some even said, "This is what the composer had in mind."

Jane Stuart Smith

Today Jane Stuart Smith is too busy living in the present to linger over the past. You see, she met God one day in the mountains of Switzerland and life has never been the same again. Before she sang with her voice; today she sings with her life. Knowing God has become such a dynamic reality that she lost concern for fame and fortune, earthy ingredients for fulfilling dreams, and got caught up in a bigger Plan. If you don't understand, you may say, "How fanatical!" or "What a waste!" but that may only be evidence that you haven't ever seen how big God is. Let me tell you about her life, and you will see for yourself what has happened.

The year was 1951 and the place Venice. Colorful posters all about the city-of-canals announced the opera *Turandot* with the leading role to be sung by the rising young American soprano, Jane Stuart Smith. This was her European debut, and the future depended on her success in singing this difficult role before an audience who had heard the best in Europe. If she were whistled and booed off this stage, it would finish her in Italy for years to come.

Her beloved and clever Maestro knew what was at stake better than Jane. Not only was her career involved, but his reputation as well. If she could live up to expectation tonight, she would capture in this one performance all of Italy, and Europe as well. He knew his pupil's ability and had worked long and carefully with her, pouring the best he had into her mind and voice. She, in turn, had come to him with an already superbly trained voice and he never ceased wondering at her willingness to work and produce beyond his expectation.

Tonight's performance was being held in St. Mark's square in an outdoor theater, in as glamorous a setting as Europe can provide. Four thousand opera lovers were waiting in the square to see and hear if the much-talked-about American really had the voice and dramatic ability to be Princess Turandot. She was dressed now in her green satin and brocade gown, with the long, lacy mantle sparkling with beads and jewels — a spectacular Chinese costume. Her long plastic, oriental fingernails were in place, and Jane was ready for the gondola ride which was part of the pageantry of Venice. She could have dressed near the theater, but that is not the way it is done in Venice. The leading lady must arrive at the theater square in a gondola.

As the gondolier steered down the last narrow canal and swished them quietly under the last bridge, Jane was overcome with the almost unbelievably romantic setting in which she was to sing — the opulent old city, the beautiful square silhouetted by a full moon. She saw the audience and heard the orchestra, and suddenly Jane Stuart Smith was ready. As the Maestro helped her out of the gondola, he saw that she was already Turandot, the beautiful, cruel princess of China.

She performed with all her voice and heart that night, and felt a thrill of triumph as she sang the last aria. The audience thundered its approval. People swarmed back stage after the last curtain call — photographers, autograph seekers, friends, friends of friends, and most important of all, an impressario from one of the largest theaters in Europe with a contract in his hand for Jane Stuart Smith to sing the same opera in Palermo. Jane Smith had made it in Europe.

Jane grew up singing. Her mother had a lovely soprano voice, and early acquainted Jane with good music. Jane loved opera even as a young girl, and tells of locking herself in her room, listening to *Tristan and Isolde*. She would walk grandly through the roles, draped in a sheet, with a lamp shade on her head, dramatizing and singing along with the recording. In her dreams she was the beautiful, poised, boney-thin prima donna, while in real life her brothers teased her that she was too fat, too loud and too clumsy.

Hometown friends in Roanoke, Virginia smile when they speak of Jane for they feel she is theirs. They knew her from the first yodle as she galloped across the lawn in her favorite cowboy suit. From her seventeenth birthday on, Roanoke knew she would be a success.

While she was a student at Hollins College in Virginia, she set her mind on a career in opera. She began studying operas and listening to recordings by the hours. She saved her allowance, rode all night on a train to New York — anything to see a real opera. She studied at Julliard School of Music in New York, and later at Tanglewood Music School in Massachusetts. In 1951 she went to Italy to study under one of the most gifted vocal teachers in the world, Maestro Ettore Verna. "Without his brilliant instruction and personal interest in my career," Jane says, "I would have been like hundreds of others who study for years, but never sing on stage."

Certainly he had wasted no time in placing her before a European audience. The Maestro was almost beside himself with joy at Jane's triumph in Venice. But success doesn't come easily in the world of opera, and the Maestro, who knew this better than anyone, was merciless in his demands on Jane. He dearly loved her and called her *Bella Salamona* (an Italian expression of tenderness, literally translated *Beautiful Salami,* which tells you a great deal about Italian values), but he could shift from the endearments of a lamb to the snarling of a lion. He picked at her about small details, he put her through grinding repetitions, groaning, weeping, storming about in a fury to get her to perform up to his standards. The more she gave out, the more potential he saw, and he drove her to perfection.

The Maestro had the lovable inconsistencies of a genius. He roared at his students that they must never smoke or even be in a place where others smoked. But the first thing he did at every lesson was to light up a cigarette. As he grew more tense, he would empty one pack after another, until the room was thick with smoke, the pianist gasping, and his pupils choking over the high notes.

Day after day it was the same, hours on end. Ten times through the same notes, with the Maestro banging with one hand against the music stand, giving it a permanent list to the portside, and wildly waving his glasses with the other hand.

"Open your mouth!"

"Stand straight."

"Smile!"

"Don't pucker your lips."

"Use your hands. Hands make the singer. Make them flow."

"Full open tone."

And finally with a trembling voice, "Sing it through once more, Cara, as though it is the most important thing in the world to you.

Then, mellowed by the music, "Fine, we'll let it go at that. *Bella Salamona,* your school days are over. From now on sing and act like a prima donna, a big prima donna. You must learn to love your voice more, Cara. Love it so much you cry inside."

And so it would go, each rehearsal, over and over again. When she sang to his satisfaction musically and emotionally, he would storm at her Italian pronunciation and tell her if she couldn't improve she should go home and sing in America. He would throw down his score, pull his hair, loosen his necktie, and shout. Jane would stand poised and calm, hopping mad inside, until she couldn't contain it any longer. Tears would come, and the Maestro, mistaking fury for passion, would feel he had gotten his point across.

When the Maestro said, "From now on opera is your god, and you're going to eat, sleep, dream, and live it," the rebel in Jane wanted to defy his control over her life. But she knew that he knew, and if she wanted success she had to listen to him. Sometimes the superficiality and make-believe of the world she lived in both on and off stage nearly suffocated her. Milan was a far cry from Virginia and central heating, and there were times when Jane wondered if it was worth it all.

Although the Italian-born Maestro was an American citizen, nearly every opera season he was back in Italy, helping one of his special pupils become successful. In Milan, he considered Signora Rolandi his best friend. Before her husband's death, the Rolandis moved in the opera world of Milan. Signora Rolandi always opened her spacious apartment to him and to his pupils and soon she became Jane's best friend as well. She cooked Italian food for Jane, corrected her pronunciation, gave her advice, protected and loved her. She was Jane's comfort after her strenuous sessions with the Maestro. It was no secret that the Maestro had favorites, and Signora Rolandi often said, "The one he likes best he almost kills." When a disheveled professor and a weary Jane arrived back home, Mrs. Rolandi's cheerful "Here come my two warriors at last!" was as welcome as the smell of garlic, onions and tomatoes coming from the kitchen. Italian perfume, Jane called it.

Jane Smith was up to the pace she kept. A tall, healthy, statuesque woman, Jane had what is known as "stage presence" both on and off stage. Her active mind not only absorbed all she was handed about the stage and opera, but she read incessantly. She had earlier resolved to read all of the five hundred classics listed in the Modern Library series, and by 1951 she was as far down the alphabet as Proust. When the Maestro said, "Rest your voice," Jane took to books. The Maestro's orders were also lights out at 10:30, stay away from drafts, avoid mountain air, curtail social engagements, and on and on. But it worked. Each time another performance was scheduled, Jane was ready and her critics recognized this.

The world of opera is cruel, which perhaps doesn't make it too much different from many other professions. Success is hard come by, and those who aspire to the top must take their share of jealous, cutting remarks from those further down the ladder. A cheap, shoddy kind of living is common for many, and scandals keep tongues wagging. Rivalry among the climbing members of a company lead to spiteful, selfish tricks to discredit others. Jane had no claim to sainthood herself, but she was often sickened by the ugly meaninglessness of it all. Even her social life was full of empty, brittle talk.

"A prize group of unhappy, grasping misfits" — that is how Jane described the opera world in her more depressed moments. "Everyone must always be young in the theater, and no one wants to face what will happen when we're old and no longer have the stage to strut on, the fans to cheer us on." When she tried discussing this with her beloved

Maestro, the talks always ended in an argument. She was told not to bother her head about such things.

"It is difficult to explain," Jane says, "but there was a gnawing, inner sense of something lacking. When I saw the work of the English sculptor, Henry Moore, I identified with his expression of this inner emptiness. His figures all have a hollowed-out part, an actual hole in the center of their being. That's how I felt."

Jane had a series of stormy sessions with the Maestro about church, religion and God. Not that Jane knew so much about any of the three, but she had been brought up to attend church. No matter where she was, she rarely missed going to church on Sunday. She sometimes wondered why she did this, but it was a vaguely comforting habit. The sermons often did little for her, and she wasn't sure exactly what she thought about God. She prayed the Lord's prayer occasionally before a trip or an important concert as a sort of talisman to cover any exigencies she might face. She had read her Bible as part of her reading program. The margins of her Old Testament were filled with the scribbled notes from lectures of religion professors in college who had described it as a collection of myths and legends. Influenced by them, she could not accept the primitive concept of God she found in its pages.

About the time she flew to Egypt for a series of appearances, Jane's uneasiness was becoming harder to cover over. The appalling contrast between her glamorous life on the stage, the sophisticated wealthy crowd with whom she sipped cocktails in some exclusive club in Cairo, and the abject poverty and stench she witnessed along the Nile raised too many depressing questions in her mind. Further, the rehearsals were difficult, with quarreling and hot tempers. Jane had many moments when she would gladly have lined up the entire company and shot them dutifully one by one. Emotionally and physically exhausted, even the praise of Cairo could not change Jane Smith's feeling that there must be more to life than this.

As she flew out of Cairo, and saw again the Nile from the

air and the vastness of the Sahara Desert, Jane Stuart Smith in one sentence came closer to finding the answer to her emptiness than she ever had before. She looked up into the sky as the plane headed across the Mediterranean and breathed out, "If there is a living God, show me."

Jane said, "It was a strange experience. I wasn't sure to whom I was speaking, but I knew I was heard. I knew there was Somebody bigger than me who could help."

One gray Sunday in Milan Jane went to the Anglican church, hoping that she would hear something to revive her heart. She sat in the back row, listening hard for some word from the minister which would give meaning to her life, but there was nothing there. The vicar's message was as empty as her conversations with Egypt's intellectuals in Cairo. During the last hymn, tears rolled down her face at her disappointment. She thought, *There probably are no answers. I'm just a hollow person.*

She left the sanctuary, lost in her thoughts. *Why did I ever bother to come? Not even the music reached me today,* Jane told herself. Her thoughts were interrupted by a wisp of a girl, saying in English,

"Excuse me, but aren't you Jane Stuart Smith? I have heard you sing several times," the girl rushed on, afraid she would be cut off, "and I think you have a marvelous voice."

Jane thanked her politely, brightened by the girl's admiration and sincerity, and turned to leave. But the girl went on. "Could I invite you to dinner?"

This was going a bit too far, and Jane was glad when her driver approached and she made the quick excuse that she was expected elsewhere. But the girl was not so easily deterred from her objective and as Jane entered the car, she asked, "Would you be able to come on Monday or Tuesday night? I . . ."

The prima donna didn't know how to graciously get out of such an open-ended invitation, but handed the girl a card and said, "Call me . . ." and drove off.

The following week she rehearsed *Norma,* Act II. She had a cold and rehearsals were a nightmare. The pressure to find some new way to be more than just any Norma left her exhausted and Jane despairingly wrote in her diary: "Voice gradually going to pieces, and my heart with it." But things were not as bad as she imagined, and after an enforced rest to recuperate from the cold, Jane's voice was stronger and sounder than before.

One night, following her recuperation, Jane's phone rang, and she answered it to find the young girl who had spoken to her at the church on the other end of the line. She had called before and left messages which Jane had ignored. At least she is persistent, thought Jane, and she accepted the invitation for the following Saturday night.

As soon as she had hung up Jane was sorry she had been such a soft-hearted idiot. What was she getting herself into? Fans were wonderful, and she had to admit she liked being important, but a dinner with a fawning hostess was a little too much. What could she possibly have in common with this church mouse? She laughed as she thought of the Maestro's word, "If you're going to break training rules and spend an evening out, make it worthwhile. Be sure it is spent with a duke or a count, or a famous conductor."

Jane went to the dinner, reluctantly, but at least she kept her word. She was welcomed by a warm, intelligent looking person who said her name was Georgia. Inside she met vivacious Maria Theresa, and her church-step friend, Anita. They ate in the kitchen, a delightful tasty buffet supper. The cozy warmth of the place and the wholesome friendship of these girls made Jane relax. This might just be a fun evening.

"It's curious the things one remembers," says Jane. "It's often the little things, rather than the more obvious things that impress you when you first meet someone. But that night one of the girls gave thanks for the food. I'm not sure which one it was, but what I'll never forget is that she really seemed to be talking to *someone* when she prayed. I was a tiny bit homesick, too, and the realization hit me pretty hard that I had not heard a table prayer since I left Virginia."

The conversation around the table was lively and interesting. Jane found herself enjoying the directness and simplicity of her hostesses. Somewhere in the conversation someone mentioned a study they were having that evening, and then explained that it was a *Bible* study and would Jane be interested in joining them. Jane assured them that she had read the Bible through, but had found it painfully dull, but yes, she would stay and listen.

Jane's good nature didn't last very long. She found herself irritated and she interrupted constantly, giving her prima donna opinions in an unpleasant, obnoxious way. Her poor manners didn't seem to upset her hostesses, however, and they listened politely to her rampage. Later, reflecting on how she had acted, Jane knew these girls had *something,* or they would have thrown her out.

Of all things, the girls invited Jane back to the next Bible study. She agreed to go, even though it caused an awful fuss with Signora Rolandi and her other opera friends. "Going to a Bible class" was ridiculous! But she did go, again and again. At one of these meetings, the class had a visitor from Switzerland. He was a professor and he spoke with a quiet authority. He told the story of how he had left his law office to become a teacher of the Bible. He said that the Bible had meant nothing to him until the day he had a personal encounter with Jesus Christ.

Jane didn't have much to say that evening. She mostly listened. Later she talked to Maria Theresa about how anyone could have a personal encounter with someone who had been dead nearly 2000 years. "It could happen to you, too, Jane," Maria Theresa said. "All you have to do is open your heart and invite him in." They were interrupted by guests who were leaving, and Jane said good-by herself and went back to Signora Rolandi's apartment.

With the Maestro back from America, Jane didn't get to many Bible studies for a long time. She had no time to even think about it because she had signed a contract to sing the lead in *Norma* near Milan in May. Jane's goal was to make Norma convincing, and she lived, ate, breathed and slept Norma. Occasionally after her strenuous sessions with the Maestro, Jane would chafe at his demands, but on the whole, it was good to be studying with him again. No one was more important in her life than he. Only sometimes she felt lonely and miles apart from him. To the Maestro, opera was life, and he could not understand why Jane sought anything more than the success she was enjoying.

In April, when Spring should have come to Milan but delayed, Jane felt she needed a respite. She called Georgia one dreary day, and asked her about the place in Switzerland that she had heard mentioned at the Bible studies. Apparently an American family named Schaeffer had a place called L'Abri where people could come and stay. It seemed a strange set-up, but Switzerland sounded good to Jane at the moment, and arrangements were made for Jane and Anita to go. Jane's main thought was to get away from the dampness and cold of Milan for Easter weekend.

Switzerland was as damp and dreary as Italy that weekend, and Jane missed seeing the charm and beauty of the breath-taking valley and mountains from this little town of Huemoz. Jane suspected that the Schaeffers were missionaries and was wary at first. But their hospitality was disarming and she forgave them for choosing so lowly an occupation. The conversation was alive and stimulating and she was completely taken off guard when Mr. Schaeffer asked her abruptly, "Jane, are you a Christian?"

No one had ever asked her that in her whole life before, and he said it as blandly as he might ask, "Are you an opera singer?" She was so stunned and embarrassed that she blurted out, "I think I am."

The hot water bottle Mrs. Schaeffer gave her didn't quite remove the chill from the bed that night, but worse was the chill around her heart. *Of course, I am a Christian,* she kept telling herself.

On Easter Sunday morning Mr. Schaeffer conducted a worship service for the guests in their family living room. Jane played the piano and sang along with the hymns. It was a good, fresh kind of service and the irritation of the previous evening dropped away. Everybody talked about God as if they knew Him at this place, and Jane tried to follow the different conversations she was hearing as she helped with dinner preparations. *What on earth was this all about?* she wondered.

Everyone at the Schaeffers enjoyed talking, and Jane, used to being at the center of the stage, sat quietly and listened. The dinner conversation was woven through with Christianity, art, music, politics, and history. These people were intelligent, convincing and happy. When Mr. Schaeffer spoke later about what a Christian really is, Jane knew why she had felt so uneasy the night before. She had thought a Christian meant simply being honest, fair, and as good as the next fellow. She was beginning to see that for the Schaeffers being a Christian meant something far deeper than this. Mr. Schaeffer referred to it as being "born again."

On Monday afternoon, Mr. Schaeffer invited Jane to take a walk with him. Conversation quickly turned to the Bible. Jane could not get over the fact that he spoke with conviction and scholarship about the unified message of the Old and New Testaments. All she had ever heard before made the Old Testament a vast collection of myths, and now she was hearing of God's plan from beginning to end. The more he talked, the more the puzzle fit together and things were making sense to her. The broken relationship between God and man had been bridged by Jesus Christ, and knowing God meant meeting Him in the person of Christ. "Suddenly I saw that the God of the Bible is the God of history and to know Him is our purpose in life," Jane says.

There on that mountainside, Jane Stuart Smith did the only thing God required of her. She believed. Believing, she felt the weight which had pressed on her so long slip away, and although she had never called it sin, she knew it to be that now. Believing, she met God in Jesus Christ. And while they stood there above the village, the fog lifted and the sun broke through, and for the first time Jane saw the loveliness of the valley, the majesty of the snowpeaks, and the wildflowers covering the hillside. What was happening to her vision of the valley was like what was happening to her heart.

Jane returned to Milan with a new treasure, almost afraid to talk about it to anyone for fear it would take away the glow of her experience. But she did speak of it, first to those who would understand. She wrote a letter to the Schaeffers, and then called the girls who had first contacted her, asking if they could change the monthly Bible study to a weekly one. Then she spoke to others about what an amazing thing it was to know God, strange news that was to reach the ears of her Maestro.

The Bible became an exciting book. In true Jane style, she equipped herself with correspondence courses, with dictionaries, maps and commentaries, and went to work to learn all she could. She worked on her studies in her dressing room before performances. She found the Bible calmed her in those anxious moments. She read boxfuls of books sent by the Schaeffers. Jane never did anything half-heartedly.

Soon after her return from Switzerland, she put the finishing touches on *Norma.* The Maestro had ignored the things he had heard about his *Bella Salamona,* hoping if he didn't speak of it her fervor would die. Jane hadn't said much to the Maestro, thinking that if she could prove to him that her singing was better because she trusted God, then he would not be against it. The Maestro was thinking, if she sings *Norma* as I think she will, she will be so much in demand she won't have time to think about religion.

The *Norma* performance was rewarded by a standing audience shouting, *"Brava! Bravissima!"* and the sweetest words of all came from the Maestro himself. He had been right. After tonight she could sing anything anywhere.

She did. Jane Stuart Smith went from success to success. But in the months ahead the serenity she had experienced after her conversion faded. She began to feel uneasy about her career, as if it was an idol with which she had to deal. Even the Maestro had the sickening fear that she had started to serve two gods. He believed a singer could have only one god — opera.

Meanwhile Jane argued in her heart that Jesus wanted His disciples in all walks of life. Yet the more she knew of God, the more shabby the opera world looked, too appealing to the flesh, too much exaltation of self. In her Bible reading she kept running across verses like, "Choose you this day whom ye will serve." Was God possibly asking her to lay her Isaac on the altar as Abraham had done?

Then the pressure of work would drive the questions out of her mind. She loved Wagner's operas. (Her Italian Maestro thought this a peculiar taste since he deemed the German's works long, loud and unromantic!) Her life dream was to sing Brunnhilde in *Die Walküre*. Now, as Brunnhilde, she went on tour throughout Italy. She sang *Tannhäuser* in Palermo, and everywhere she went her audience declared that they had never heard it sung better.

When the Schaeffer's daughter was married, Jane sang at the wedding. (Mrs. Schaeffer describes it as the loveliest wedding gift she could have given.) Dr. Martyn Lloyd-Jones of Westminster Chapel in London performed the marriage ceremony, and Jane was intrigued to hear that he had given up a successful career as a medical doctor to become a preacher. She thought of what people must have said about him, the agony he must have gone through in reaching his decision. Yet Jane was impressed that he was such a joyful, purposeful man. Were some people given a special gift of faith that they could so easily give up something so precious to them? Jane concluded the Christian life was no bed of roses.

Jane had gone back to Roanoke to sing *The Messiah* in her home town. Now on her way back to Vienna to study German, she transferred to a smaller two-engine plane bound for Geneva so that she might visit the Schaeffers at L'Abri. Jane was reading Psalm 119, and paused to look out the window at the mountain peaks below. At that moment, one of the engines missed a beat and then stopped. Within seconds the other engine struggled and likewise died. The silence was awful, and the mountains seemed to clutch at the plane. Almost immediately the stewardess came on the intercom, and with a voice trained to absolve panic, she gave the passengers directions for an emergency landing.

The verse Jane had been reading in Psalm 119 at the moment she looked out of the window was verse 175: "Let my soul live, and it shall praise thee." In the ominous silence of those moments, as the plane lost altitude rapidly, Jane faced up to the fact that she might shortly be ushered into God's presence. She thought about what a tawdry life she had to present before God, made some sharp adjustments in her values, and cried out to God, "Lord, give me back my life and I will give it to you."

At the last possible moment, one of the engines started to sputter, coughed and then came on with a loud, steady sound, and the pilot, with great skill, maneuvered the crippled plane to Geneva with one engine. No one on that plane is likely to forget that flight.

Call it happenstance. Say it was "just one of those things." Recount all the stories you have heard of promises made in dire moments. None of these would affect Jane. An experience like this is a personal thing and only the person involved knows its significance.

Later in Vienna Jane did what she knew she must do. When she had given her superb performance of *Die Walküre* in Naples the previous May, she could not have borne it if she had known that was to be her last performance on stage. She was willing to give up opera *someday,* but not until she had established herself in the coveted role of the leading Brunnhilde of the year. Now she did what she knew was right, and asked God to help the people so dear to her to understand.

As she walked to the opera house, Satan reminded her of what she was giving up every step of the way. Her opera manager was aghast. He pulled out a file from his brief case and began to read her the headlines about her performances. Then he listened to her story and wept. She wrote to her parents telling them about what she had told God in the airplane, and to Signora Rolandi.

The Maestro was the hardest. She got as far as "My dear

Maestro . . ." several times, and then broke down. Three days later she mailed the letter to him. It was months before the Maestro could even hear the name *Bella Salamona* without tears.

If anyone had ever told Jane Stuart Smith that she would work so hard to achieve her goal and then give it up, she would have never believed it. More accurately, Jane would say today, "God changed my goal." She doesn't believe this dramatic action is wholesale advice from God for everyone. She just knew that Jane Smith was faced with serving two gods, and she couldn't do it. She had to choose.

Today Jane works with the Schaeffers at L'Abri, helping communicate to the scores of students and visitors who come to the little mountain town of Huemoz because they have heard that somebody there knows God. She lives in a chalet just below the Schaeffers with Betty Carlson, and Signora Rolandi is often with her. If you could see her conduct a lively Bible study in Italian for a group of weekend visitors from Milan, or walk along the mountainside with one of the guests in deep conversation, you would know that Jane has found her place. If you could know the people whose lives have been changed by their contact with Jane Stuart Smith in this role, you would understand that her energies are wisely invested.

She still sings; the valley often echoes back her magnificent voice. But it's a new song.

8

Karen Howe

Brown-eyed, vivacious Karen Elvgren Howe, once a rebel against God, is now a disciple of Jesus Christ. She is also the wife of John Howe, a student at Yale Divinity School and member of the staff of Inter-Varsity Christian Fellowship in New England. Kari, as John calls her, is living proof of her own words: "The Christian life is incredibly dynamic."

I DON'T KNOW WHY I noticed it that morning. It wasn't a special Sunday at all. But the words were suddenly so vivid, and even as I spoke them another part of me considered them in a detached manner. "We have erred and strayed from Thy ways like lost sheep . . . there is no health in us . . . but Thou, O Lord, have mercy upon us miserable offenders . . ."

Lost sheep? Miserable offender? Mercy? No, not me. I was not lost, nor miserable, and mercy I did not want nor need.

Karen Howe

I was sixteen, the oldest child of wealthy parents, living in a lovely home in a North Shore suburb of Chicago. That morning I was attending church with a friend, as I had done with some regularity since I had been confirmed two years earlier. But for the first time I actually heard the words of the Confession I had long known by heart. I left the church that morning with the excitement of a newborn rebel. If Christianity involved admittance of sin with the consequent burden of guilt and the need to beg for mercy from a displeased God, I would have none of it. The sudden freedom was intoxicating, and I did not attend church again without scorn for all who worshiped there.

This rebelling against my Father in heaven had been preceded by years of resentment against my earthly father. I felt unable to please this rather domineering, extremely successful, awesome individual, and my failure to feel loved and accepted by him forced me to protect my sore and wounded ego by refusing to try any longer. I disdained his efforts to establish a friendly relationship and sought affection elsewhere, primarily from the young men who began to seek my company. But while I pursued male attentions and was desperate without them, I held my own emotions in a tight ball of fearful restraint. I knew that honest love involved a vulnerability I could not face. With other teenagers from wealthy homes who had too much money, too much freedom, and too little chaperonage, I defied my father's efforts to curb my excessive dating and often participated in irresponsible and unbridled behavior. I was neither willing nor able to relinquish the social excitement I craved, so I chose to deny the God and the Law which called my compulsive behavior "sin."

I began my freshman year at college as a self-centered, self-confident, emotionally immature girl. My social calendar was never empty, and my academic work was well above average. I studied the Bible under a professor who approached it as poetry and legend, and I became increasingly convinced that God was man's creation, and not visa versa. Whatever need it was that led human kind to invent the God-concept, it was certainly no need of mine. I castigated with long, verbose arguments any fellow student daring to admit to a trace of Christian faith in my presence.

I had selected a college in California, primarily to get as far away from home as possible. However, an alert aunt living near the college town got wind of my increasingly undisciplined behavior, and notified my family. My father informed me that my sophomore year would be spent nearer home.

As I had little to say in the matter, I attended the following year an extraordinarily expensive co-educational institution three hours from home. Immediately I formulated two goals: to pledge a good sorority, and to quickly find the male attention which I needed if I was to maintain a sense of well-being. Dominating male members of the species seemed to be a compulsive drive within me, and I was never satisfied until I felt I had at least one under my control. I managed to accomplish both of these goals within a few months, but was increasingly dissatisfied and unstable, often spending whole afternoons in the local college bar sullenly drinking bourbon and 7 up.

My life began to find renewed purpose when I enrolled in a political science course under a professor of radically right-wing orientation. I devoured several of his courses, and soon possessed a crusading spirit akin to his. I felt chosen to work to save my country from the inroads being made upon her vital institutions by creeping socialism and communism. My love of independence enabled me to identify with the laissez-faire economic theories which were described as the heart and core of "Americanism"; the authoritarian aspects of my personality responded to my teacher's demand that all communists and fellow travelers be exposed and punished.

I soon discovered, to my dismay, that faith in God had been a major factor in the development of American ideals of individual liberty and responsibility. With reluctance I accepted this, but God remained only a philosophic necessity to me. Certainly I did not see Him as a personal Lord with whom individuals had to deal. Somehow, though, I was never as hostile to religion as I had been; a basic barrier within me had fallen and God became tolerable.

That spring my disregard for college social regulations resulted in an official request that I not return to school the following fall. I went home that summer with a hard knot of desperation forming within me. What could I do? I was convinced that America was on the verge of annihilation and no one seemed to care. My own future seemed shattered since continued education now appeared unlikely. My drinking, chain smoking and excess nervous energy seemed to be the cause of terrible headaches which I grew to dread.

My patriotic concern was the only avenue where some improvement might be possible. I poured myself into political activities. I urged my parents to gather their friends together so I might enlighten them to the dangers threatening our country. Incredibly presumptuous as I was, the friends did gather, and did listen to my lectures and chalk-talks, and we soon had an active anti-communist cell group eagerly trying to save America from destruction from within. We wrote letters to congressmen, invited out-of-town experts to address citizens' groups, and we tried to interest our lethargic neighbors. But there was always the nagging fear that we were not doing enough and could never do enough to help the situation.

At the end of the summer, I was offered a job by the editor-owner of a very conservative daily newspaper in town, and for the first time my life blossomed. This was augmented by the social security I was enjoying at the time. I had a faithful boyfriend, a twenty-nine year old architectural draftsman who had left his job in the college community to be closer to me. He was working as a cattle drover for a nearby ranch, and was looking for something more promising. He had a history of difficulty in finding and keeping jobs. However, he did seem to love me and I had him well within my control, and that was where my concern ended.

God did not let me enjoy this false security for long. Although I refused to take Him seriously, He was seriously at work in the hearts of a couple in our cell group. Once active church people, they had for many years been inactive and were no longer even church members. Our discussions had driven them to a renewed faith in Jesus Christ, perhaps because they, too, sensed our inability to provide real solutions to the problems we were discussing. They joined a good church and began to pray for me and others in our group. They were persuaded that Jesus Christ was the answer to the world's needs, to America's dilemma, and to each individual life. Needless to say, I was horrified.

"How can you *possibly* believe Jesus was God?" I once asked them, furious that they should expound such an incredibly narrow faith. I will never forget their answer, so gently given: "He said He was, and either He was telling the truth or He was lying." There were no intellectual arguments, no sign of doubt on their part — nothing I could clutch at and use as a weapon to make them change their minds. I could not escape these words, and when the storm began to hit my life with hurricane force, I remembered them in desperate hope.

The first gusts had already hit when my college plans had collapsed. The next blows came when I learned that my boyfriend, with whom marriage seemed likely, had been married three times previously and had hundreds of dollars of debts strewn across the country in a trail behind him. This was the man upon whom I depended. What, I thought frantically, would our future be like?

One night shortly after receiving this crushing news, I found myself unable to sleep. Fears crowded in on me. I began to consider the sorry condition of my life. I was a noisy personality, sick with the need for affection and the need to dominate others, unable to enjoy a truly unselfish relationship with anyone. Panic gripped me as I looked into a future which held no hope for educational advancement, and seemed, therefore, to point only to a marriage with an irresponsible divorcee whom I would probably end up supporting and, eventually, divorcing. I did not have the inner security to let go of my relationship with this man, and nothing seemed likely to provide the miracle I knew would be needed if any of the other conditions were to be improved.

How clearly I remember that night. I sat cross-legged on the floor of my bedroom, listening to the night sounds outside. I could hear the waves slapping against our dock and the crickets' conversation. In numb detachment I pondered the number of aspirin it would take to destroy my life — I doubted that we had anything more potent than that in the house. I stared at the ceiling, and from somewhere the thought came: *If You are real, help me . . . become real to me.*

Hope against hope, what if He were? What if He could be so real that He could fill the emptiness and still the fear? What if they were right and I had been wrong about God all along? I knew that if God were real I could find in Him the strength to give up my relationship with my boyfriend. But God would have to be very big to provide me with that sort of security. I cried out that night to what I dared not yet believe in — in the vague hope that perhaps there was a One behind the great philosophic X I had so long called *god.*

Given the reality of God, all things are possible. With utmost love the Father I had refused to acknowledge for so long worked toward me through the only available channel, my Christian friends. After much persuasion I agreed to go with them to church one Sunday morning, simply because the minister was going to speak on communism and I was smugly sure that I knew far more about the subject than he. I arrived, carefully dressed, gay and critical, yet inside somehow timid and afraid. I had never been in a church that did not resemble a cathedral, and have always felt (and still do feel) most at home in the formal beauty of a highly liturgical service. I found myself in a small, casual church, and its simplicity quite disarmed me. As those about me opened battered old hymnals and began to sing wonderfully melodious, joyous gospel tunes I became even more unsettled. For the first few verses I sang with them, but I was soon unable to continue. Something inside me, something that had managed to remain soft and simple, responded to the amazing words of those songs and to the Spirit moving among those faith-filled people.

I began to cry. I wept, utterly abashed, but unable to regain my composure. Why, these people were singing about a God they knew, a Person whom they loved and who loved them, a wonderful, approachable God, full of promises and life and hope. I had not known that I was hungry, and here I was, tasting Food for which I had always been yearning. The Holy Spirit of God touched me and I knew that I was loved.

During the following week I decided never to return to that potent place. I was ashamed and confused at my public tears. And distrustful. What if it had all been silly emotionalism? What had made me so sure that God was there? But I did return, and I knew without a doubt that I had found One with whom I did not need to pretend, because He knew all about me — all about my insecurity, my rebellion, my sin, my need for love and my fear of giving it. In the following weeks I opened my heart to Him, a little at a time, as I became increasingly safe in the assurance that He would never reject me. I am still learning the wonder of being loved regardless. God loved me for myself alone, until I dared to trust the Lover and yield my weary, defensive self to His care, once and for all.

Several weeks after my initial experience of God's grace in that Sunday morning service I publicly committed my life into the hands of Jesus Christ. I was filled with a deep need to learn as much as possible about my new Lord and the life He was opening up to me. I drank great draughts of God's love. Hungry hours were spent devouring the Scriptures and delighting in the exciting tales told me by older Christians of the miracles of God's leading and God's healing in their lives. From the very first I learned that our God is a God of miracles.

But best of all, I learned more about Jesus Christ, God's greatest gift. I discovered the Cross . . . and Easter. I realized that at a point in history Jesus had died for *my* sin and it was His death that had made my precious forgiveness by the Father possible. He had promised the Holy Spirit to His disciples, to comfort and nurture them after His death, and here I was nineteen centuries later, a young disciple, enjoying the new life which the Spirit brings to every believer.

One of the most delightful truths of all for me became the promise of Jesus' return to earth. Then everyone shall see Him, the crucified, despised Son of God, in all His kingly beauty and glory. Every knee shall bow before Him, and those who trusted Him will be with Him in a more real and intimate way than is ever possible during this life. Jesus will then establish the kingdom of God on earth and I knew that this was the answer to the problem of communism and poverty and every other human difficulty which had troubled me personally and intellectually.

I was shortly to begin experimenting in God's guidance and grace myself. I experienced release and renewal in many areas of my personality. One of God's first steps was to lead me to ask my father's forgiveness. I saw for the first time that much of the fault in our strained relationship was my own. I broke off my ties with my boyfriend, and knew the relief and cleansing which comes when one obeys God in some area of life. The Holy Spirit was so real to me that my loneliness was not overwhelming.

I began to feel that God would have me return to college, but I did not see how this would be possible. Hopefully I wrote to Ohio Wesleyan University for an application. I read it with concern, noting that I had to indicate whether or not my standing was good at the school I had previously attended. I wrote to the Dean of Women at the college I had left, and told her quite frankly that since being asked to leave I had become a Christian, a new person in Jesus Christ. Could she tell me what my status was so I might honestly fill in my application to Ohio Wesleyan? She replied in a lovely letter that I was free to say that my standing was good and any derogatory remarks about my social behavior would not be mentioned in my transcript record. Joyfully I applied to Ohio Wesleyan and was accepted as a junior transfer student.

During my two years there I did not date. God in His

wisdom broke my dependence upon masculine attention. I also learned that "in me dwelleth no good thing," as St. Paul describes it. As a perfectionist I had always found it difficult to acknowledge imperfections in my life, and as a Christian I wanted God to make me perfect overnight. My pride took a beating during those years, but I stopped being afraid of facing sin in my life. This was a very important and stabilizing period for me.

Since then I have come to rely entirely on the fact that I am acceptable to God because of Christ's merit, and never my own. God is changing me, refining me into His image, but my relationship to Him never rests upon the degree of Christ-likeness I attain. Christian virtue is developed slowly, I learned. As I face my sins and failures with good-humored faith and keep obedience to His Word my prime goal, God gives me victory over formerly rebellious areas of my nature. The Christian life is incredibly dynamic.

Upon graduation from Ohio Wesleyan I was granted a graduate fellowship in the field of International Relations at the University of Connecticut. When I arrived on campus I looked up the chapter of Inter-Varsity Christian Fellowship, to which I had been introduced at Ohio Wesleyan. I knew I would find fellow Christians there. At the first IVCF meeting of the year I met John. In the security of John's love I slowly learned to care for another person without hidden motive and to risk the hurt that is a possibility in every love relationship. We both prayed that God would guide our romance, and we soon knew without any question that it was His will for us to be married. I am amazed that God called to the joys and responsibilities of marriage one who had so avoided love and had so misused relationships with men in the past.

We were married one year after we met, and I am so glad that I allowed God to choose my husband for me. Learning to love has become the most exciting part of marriage and of living for me, although it is not easy. God must often use difficult circumstances and difficult people to rub away the self in me so that He might love others through me. Probably my most difficult problem will always be my strong, independent personality. Learning self-control, submission and obedience has not come naturally, and both God and husband have been very patient with me.

Our tomorrows are God's. We both know that we will have, individually, and as a couple, troubles and tensions, perhaps deep sorrows. We are not immune to those difficulties that beset all members of our fallen race. But we are both persuaded that nothing is immune to the touch of God. He overcame so many barriers to reach me in His love that I am sure no circumstances are beyond His control. The main source of strength in our lives is the sure knowledge that we belong to God and that our lives are directed and sustained by Him.

9

Shelley Mydans

Shelley Mydans' bestseller historical novel, Thomas, *will take you on a walk through Thomas Becket's life with superb skill. Now I am faced with the task of taking you on a walk through Shelley's life, in much briefer form and with much less skill. But I would be pleased if you could know, in even a small way, the wonder of what God has done for Shelley Mydans, overshadowing her life until He could break through to her.*

LIFE is so beautifully simple when you are young, Shelley Mydans thought, as she pounded the pavements of New York. Grubbing for a living in the 1930's in a hard, impersonal city was a world away from the delights of her carefree childhood. She was unprepared for the poverty and sadness she witnessed. No one had given her answers for this kind of a terrible world.

They talked about these things, Shelley and her intellectual young friends, in the big city in the East. The world was cruel and heartless, and all her idealistic reasonings cried out against the unfairness of life for some. She joined the liberal United Front Movement, believing it contained a possible political solution for America.

Shelley had grown up in a happy home with all the security that loving and being loved can give. Her mother was an Emersonian Unitarian; her father had been a Quaker, but over the years he had become a Unitarian of a very intellectual sort. They had stopped going to church when Shelley was a small child, and a humanistic attitude permeated the family thinking. Man could work out his own way and was really becoming much cleverer than he had earlier been thought to be. Her father was a professor at Stanford University in California, and Shelley grew up as the younger sister of three brothers in a free thinking era on the edge of a university campus.

God is love, Shelley had been taught. Creation has always been awesome to Shelley, who loves the out-of-doors. God was linked with creation, which was good and great and beautiful, so God must be that way, too. When she felt thankful, she thanked Him. The world was safe and happy.

Shelley majored in English at Stanford, where some of the basics which have led to the excellence of *Thomas* were instilled in her. She was exposed to the writings of great men and great thoughts, and while she dutifully compared their philosophies, she was left with men's ideas about men. Shelley did not give her personal philosophy of life much thought during college days. If she had been challenged to do so, she might have protested on the basis of her lack of evidence and experience. She left the serious thinking about God until much later in life.

Later, working in New York, she joined the staff of *Life* magazine where she met Carl Mydans, now well-known *Life* photographer and writer, whom she later married. In 1938, twenty-four years old, Shelley was sent with her husband to Finland to cover the trouble brewing in Europe. Hitler's Nazism bore portents of evil in a blatant display of fanaticism, military build-up and anti-semitism.

The Mydans crisscrossed Europe, often working alone on

individual assignments, getting together when they could to discuss what they were seeing. Americans put their feet up and smoked their pipes in the comfort of their own living rooms, reading the Mydans' account in *Life* of the devious political drama unfolding in Europe, but it all seemed so far away. To Shelley Mydans, seeing the tensions and the tempo of life in Europe firsthand, it was not so far away. It was the stuff out of which World War II would come, and they tried to tell this to contented Americans.

I suppose if you always stay in the parlor you don't have to find answers for what you see on the streets. Shelley wasn't given the protection of that kind of life. After their European assignment, the Mydans were sent to the interior of China to cover the Sino-Japanese war. It was an undeclared war, but the Japanese had swept into the country and now controlled many of China's major ports and cities. The world was sending little aid and sympathy to the plight of the Chinese — millions of them starving as a result of the economic stranglehold Japan held on the country. The Mydans went there to report the story to the American people.

Shelley could not have been prepared for the shock of western China. She says, "Flying in from Hong Kong was like flying into a world of agony, corrupt government and human need." To an American, accustomed to seeing every effort made to relieve human suffering, the sheer magnitude of the misery she saw overwhelmed her. Where would anyone begin?

Squalor, hunger and disease lined the streets and met her at every corner. Wandering the streets, Shelley ached inside for these people. This was no mere contemplation of need in an abstract form. These were real, living people caught in a hellish plot spawned by corruption and greed. Anger, sorrow, disgust and love washed over her in such a confusing mixture that it was hard to describe what she was seeing. Those hands stretched out as she passed by tugged at her heart — the sometimes mute pleas for help or the cry for alms. She suffered over the man with the open leprous sores; the old woman with dreadful evidences of malnutrition; the young mother with pleading eyes, a baby at her breast, holding out her hand for alms. There were too many of them.

On one occasion an old man, lying on a dirty mat, ragged and filthy and obviously ill, caught Shelley's attention as she walked down the street. A tin cup for alms stood on the corner of his mat, but he was not crying for a gift. He looked more like he was about to die. She could not walk on by. What could she do? She did the only thing she knew to do: she dropped a few coins in his cup. Then as she stood there, he convulsed and died.

The awful hurt of this brief incident remains in Shelley today. She hated herself for giving only a few coins; she argued with herself about what more she could have done. Today she says, "I knew the thing that man needed most was to die in somebody's arms. He needed to know some human being cared, that someone loved him. And I gave him only coins, not myself or my love."

No one with a sensitive spirit is ever the same after experiences like these. Shelley agonized over human responsibility. Given a humanist philosophy, what was the solution? She knew nothing else.

Near the end of 1941 the Mydans were caught in Manila when the Japanese successfully invaded the Philippines, and were taken prisoners. Eventually they were shipped to Shanghai for internment, possibly because of who they were. While interned, Shelley contracted an eye disease which threatened her sight — in view of all that had already transpired, the last straw.

Shelley didn't know a personal God who cared about people's eyesight. But God knew about Shelley and He did care. By some strange outworking of circumstances, the Japanese arranged for her to receive treatment from a Nazi German eye specialist in Shanghai. During the course of the treatment she was given the freedom of the city and had unusual opportunities to see and hear what was taking place outside the camp. Again the tragedy on the streets broke her heart. When the eye infection cleared, she voluntarily rejoined her husband in the POW camp.

Looking back on her internment, Shelley comments on the fact that many missionaries were also in the POW camp. One might suppose that in such extreme privation she might either have had a great longing to know God herself, or that she might have been stimulated to at least consider Him by the missionaries interned with her. But such was not the case. Shelley was simply being badly bruised by human need. She was too numb and too busy staying alive to ask questions. When she did begin to ask, it was not, "*Who* is the answer?" but "*Why*?" Yet it was the beginning of her search.

After nearly two years of internment, the Mydans were repatriated and sent home on an exchange ship in 1943. She wrote *The Open City* upon her return, based on her experiences as a prisoner of war.

Scarred by what she had seen abroad, Shelley Mydans tried to sort out the pieces of life in the next years. She began to see the flaws in humanism as a workable philosophy of life. "The heart of the humanist," Shelley says today, "is terribly arrogant. It has self as the beginning, the end and the meaning of existence. Consequently, it offers no hope."

The Mydans now had two growing children, and Shelley felt the strain of not knowing what to give them as basic teaching about life. She was driven beyond herself, beyond mankind, to the great God "out there."

Her first experience with a personal God who knew her and cared about her problems came one day when she had been facing a difficult problem in her life. She had been moping around the house, feeling sorry for herself, trying to reason out a solution. It had been a dull day and she longed to escape the dreariness she felt. She decided to go for a drive in hopes of gaining a fresh point of view. Self-pity followed her down the road, however, as it often does, and she could not seem to shake it.

At the peak of her despair, all at once it was as if a voice said, "Shelley, you have forgotten to give thanks."

That was God, Shelley thought. Thankfulness drives a person to God and gives a new perspective. She knew it was He and she began to increasingly feel a need for a deep personal faith. Perhaps God was knowable in a way she hadn't appreciated before.

The Mydans were living in England at this time. Shelley sometimes read to the children from Charles Dickens' *A Child's History of England.* One night she read about Thomas à Becket, the son of a London merchant who became the good friend and chancellor of King Henry II and eventually the Archbishop of Canterbury. Thomas was murdered in Canterbury Cathedral in 1170 — a strange end for an archbishop. Charles Dickens pictured Thomas as power-hungry, a schemer for the throne of England.

In a visit to Canterbury some time before, Shelley had been attracted to the story of Thomas Becket. Now she stopped reading and discussed Thomas with the children. Was Dickens' account of this man true, or was it colored by his times? *I would like to find out more about what really happened,* she told the children that night. That was the germ idea for the project which was to occupy much of the next ten years of Shelley's life.

A conversation with Anya Seton, the noted historical novelist, fed Shelley's interest in Becket. Traveling in France, she was further stimulated to delve into the historical detail of Becket's life. Source material was surprisingly plentiful, she found. One source led her to another, and she was swept into the current of medieval intrigue, living in the life and times of Becket.

Shelley's own spiritual pilgrimage paralleled her research and writing of this book. She lived in the world of twelfth-century England, in which phrases from the Vulgate Bible were part of daily language. She found herself striving to understand the church, its powers, its message. Thomas was a victim of the church-throne struggle and Shelley must know something of the emotions and pressures of the conspiracy of kings and bishops. She began to read the Bible, trying to get inside of her characters to discover their passions and temptations in the light of the teachings of Christ.

Her own need for formal religious teaching heightened at this time and she began to worship regularly at St. Bartholomew the Great, a large Anglican church in London. Shelley had been brought up outside of the church, any church. Now she read with keen interest the words in the prayer book and the Apostle's Creed. She was moved by the phrases "I believe . . ." — strong statements to make unless she really did believe.

Shelley mulled over the phrases of the Creed, seeking the meaning of each in the light of the research she was doing. She discussed it with her friends, some of whom regularly attended worship on Sunday. They seemed to be able to recite the creed quite glibly. However, when asked about its validity, they said, "Oh, don't worry about that. It's just part of the ritual."

Shelley Mydans was too honest for that. If she was going to repeat it, then she was going to mean it when she said, "I believe. . . ." She remembered the words of Abelard which her father often quoted: *God also gave us human intellect.* And while she used that intellect, God worked in her heart to convince her of truth. For truth is perceived ultimately by faith. A long struggle over phrases and words ensued before Shelley came to the conviction that the creed she repeated was Truth.

Who can say how God uses all of our experiences, our doubts, our queries, our reading to make an impact on the spirit? God was meshing many threads together in Shelley's experience.

One dreary London day Shelley was hanging up clothes in the basement of their home. Her mind had been arguing over the problem of human suffering, and her spirit was agonizing sympathetically with her thought processes. She had been reading Camus on the subject, and had recently come face to face with the concept of the Fall in Genesis. Pushing the clothespins over the wet clothes on the line, she suddenly cried out to God for some answer. Overcome with the awfulness of man's sin, of the loathsomeness of her own self, she said aloud, "O God, how can You forgive us?"

God's answer was such a loving voice of forgiveness that it is difficult to describe. The basement seemed flooded with love. "Of course, I forgive. That's what the cross is all about." Whether the words were actually spoken aloud or not, they seemed that way to Shelley. But more than that, it was the voice of One who loved Shelley Mydans in particular. "Then," said Shelley, "I knew that God was not just the great Creator way out there. He was also Jesus Christ, and He loved and forgave me."

From out of the past came a memory of her mother taking her to visit a young mother with a new baby. Her mother never spoke openly about faith or God, leaving Shelley to discover these for herself, yet had been bothered by tragedies in her own world of the 1929 era. She was greatly refreshed by this visit to the new baby and its mother.

"Did you hear the loving way she spoke to that baby?" she said to Shelley, then a teen-ager. "If there were a God He would speak that way."

Shelley now knew this to be true. She had heard *Him* speak *to her* that way, and His name was Jesus Christ. It was a great day when Shelley Mydans met God in the person of Jesus Christ, and let Him into the Godhead.

One of Shelley's favorite quotations comes from Blaise Pascal, and it came to her as the voice of Jesus comforting her during her search for God: "You would not be seeking Me if you had not found Me." After she had committed herself to God, Shelley said she felt flooded with life. She experienced His comfort, as well as His love. Suddenly even death seemed different. She was given a new concept of what was involved in the glory of God.

"The humanist's works are an end in themselves," she said, "and are basically selfish. I believe that is what drove me to become a Christian. I couldn't bear to live that way. He wants us to live beyond ourselves for His glory. There is no way out of the human dilemma apart from God. We are born condemned to death, and He offers Life."

It is not easy for Shelley Mydans to speak of her faith. There's a bit of New England Puritanism in her that finds it difficult to speak about deep emotions. "From my background, there are two sacred subjects," she says, "sex and religion.

But I want to share my faith when it helps others." Sensitive and honest, Shelley has a heart-warming humility about her faith. She feels the strength is all on God's side, not hers. She often disappoints herself by neglecting His fellowship, and leaving undone things which should be done, and senses more keenly than most the tragedy of not living out one's beliefs.

Shelley's spiritual awareness is revealed in her writing of *Thomas.* Thomas Becket is faced with the temptation to use spiritual power to serve a worldly cause when the King insists that Thomas be both Chancellor of the kingdom and Archbishop of the kingdom of God. It is a temptation familiar to many who try to serve Christ in *this* world. Christ spoke knowingly about this when He said, "You cannot serve God and mammon."

As Thomas prepares for his consecration as bishop, the implication of the king's appointment to this role is suddenly clear and he hears God speak to him.

> "What is this evil thing the king wants of you?" And Thomas answered, with no pretense, no thought, an answer from a depth within himself he had not known, words that surprised him when he heard: "He wants me to deny you, Lord."[1]

And it is both Shelley Mydans and the faithful Prior Robert who say to Thomas,

> "Presumption leads men deliberately to credit to themselves the things we all know well are God's. This is an arrogance far graver and more perilous than ignorance, in that it sets God's gifts at nought. Pride is indeed the greatest of all evils, since it leads us to use God's gifts as though they were our own by natural right, and to usurp the glory due to the bestower for what we have received."[2]

Prior Robert's later words, " 'I think God is His own

---

[1]Shelley Mydans, *Thomas,* p. 290. Copyright © 1965 by Shelley Mydans. Reprinted by permission of Doubleday & Company, Inc.
[2]*Ibid.,* p. 393.

champion,' " are borne out in Shelley's life, for God broke into her life with indisputable evidence of His reality and character.

One catches the flavor of her own conversion experience when she writes of Thomas' experience:

> And for the first time a dreadful clarity came on him, and in a little voice, full of surprise, dismay, he said aloud: "Why I am loathsome!"
>
> "NEVERTHELESS, I LOVE."
>
> Whose voice was that? . . .
>
> How shattering, yet how fulfilling, to feel love for the first time.[3]

Since completing the writing of *Thomas,* Shelley Mydans has been an active participant in a weekly neighborhood Bible study group in Larchmont, New York, where she lives now. I met her first in this setting, in an eager, spirited discussion of the third chapter of James. Her concern for spiritual reality in her own life was evident not only in her contributions to the discussion, but in her application of the truth to life. The Bible speaks to her and is excitingly contemporary.

She makes no pretense at having the answers all worked out, but she tackles the problems with intellectual honesty and thoroughness as they come up, much as she did her research for Thomas Becket. One of the things which amazes her most is the fact that God uses such *human* men to accomplish his purposes. "The Old Testament," she said, "is full of imperfect men whom God used. This is the glory of it all." We talked together that day about Abraham, called by God out of Ur of the Chaldees, and were excited by his faith.

Shelley comments that one of the things which drew her to orthodox Christianity was the fact of the Resurrection. As a Unitarian, she had skimmed over Easter, never really facing its implications. She was weary of hearing the swoon theory and all of the other more implausible theories used to explain away the Resurrection, feeling the historical evidence of those

---

[3]*Ibid.,* p. 394.

who saw a resurrected Lord is more valid. If God be God, then the Resurrection is no problem. This is the dynamic of Christianity — a living Lord, for whom the disciples risked everything, even life itself. "As intellectual as I might like to think I was," she commented, "I could not explain what I knew to be historically true in any other way."

We talked together about the rich young ruler to whom Jesus said, "Sell all that you have and distribute to the poor" (Luke 18:18-30). Shelley understands the principle Jesus was getting at in this — that the rich young man couldn't have two gods — his money and Jesus Christ — that he had to make a choice. But she is too honest and searching to leave it there. She is one of the few people I've ever met who wonders seriously if Jesus might be asking her literally to do this. She wants to face up to Him honestly about this.

And that is what makes Shelley Mydans so refreshing to know. She doesn't think she is anybody when it comes to spiritual things, but she has the one thing most precious in God's sight — an open, believing heart. And she speaks a great truth when she says, "I feel like I've been found by God." When you read her book *Thomas,* remember that God found her while she was writing it.

Intermission

One day in the middle of writing this book I heard Donald Ewing, pastor and friend, talk to a group of students about the practical implications of knowing Jesus Christ.

Seated around the fireplace in the lodge at Cedar Campus that night were eager university students who wanted to know what it really meant to give your life to God. Donald Ewing was talking about the beauty of a Christ-filled life, and he used his mother to illustrate his point.

As I listened I thought, *Here is a woman no one here will ever know. He hasn't even told us her name. She's no longer on earth, and only those who loved her will remember much about her. Someday in the years to come one of her descendants may find her picture in some dusty attic and say, "Who is she?" They may never know how her life affected theirs.* It struck me that this is the future of us all.

I couldn't help thinking that from this vantage point only one thing counted about her life — that one day in a country church in Illinois this woman had come to trust Christ and had lived the rest of her life letting His life be seen in hers.

She probably wasn't perfect. No one on earth is. But the fragrance of knowing God was evident in her daily life, and others recognized it. Her son could "rise up and call her blessed" tonight, and vibrantly alive young men and women could get a glimpse of reality in a world where synthetic people are so common.

This is the story he told:

Mother was a Christian. I know because she bore the unmistakable marks of one who believed and lived a life in harmony with Christ.

She grew up on an Illinois farm almost a century ago. Life was simple then and faith was a clear-cut, straight-forward thing as it was taught and preached in the little country Dunkard church she attended. One received Christ as one's Saviour and then one lived with Christ as the Lord of life. That was the germinal dynamic of the victorious life I knew so well as I grew under the luminous shadow of her dedicated life.

She was frail, and yet she did all of her own housework in a large house up to the time of her death. She was one of the gentlest people who ever lived and yet she would have contested to the death for those she loved. She was modest and genuinely embarrassed by recognition. She was Martha in service, but Mary in affection.

One incident illustrates her level of practical Christian living in a dramatic way. I must have been eight or possibly ten years old at the time, but the details are sharp in my memory.

The neighbors in the little house next door were a sorry lot. They were gossipy and malicious, noisy and quarrelsome. The children were addicted to the appropriation of the property of others — which is a gentle way of saying that they were a pack of junior-size thieves. Collectively they were a thorn in the flesh of the neighborhood, perhaps more to my mother than to anyone else, for she was such a loving person.

On our land but close to, and shading, their kitchen window was the most miserable skeleton of a peach tree that anyone ever saw. Every spring the gnarled old tree would, with great effort, gather together all of its little store of strength and produce a few leaves, a few blossoms. In due season the blossoms would develop into tiny, hard green peaches that never matured. They were good for only one thing — throwing. You can guess who threw them and where. It had always been so, the tree was so completely unproductive that Mother decided to have it cut down and put flowers in its place.

It wasn't long before word of her decision reached the neighbors. They rushed over to plead with her to permit the old tree to stand because it was the only shade that they had on their kitchen. Their kitchen had a flat roof, and it was exposed to the merciless Illinois sun. It was a tempting picture, those rascals sweltering in their doubly-heated kitchen. There was certainly poetic justice in it; they had turned the heat on us often enough, and one could easily be tempted to see a prophetic element in the situation. But Mother was a Christian and believed that she ought to act like one. (Now *that* is a radical idea!) She said, "Of course I will leave the tree," and she did.

When spring came that year something wonderful had happened to the tree. Those bony, gaunt, old limbs disappeared in a great cloud of blossoms. The blossoms developed into the tiny, hard, green peaches that we had known across the years, and then, wonder of wonders, they matured and became wonderful, sweet, delicious fruit. There were so many peaches that we had to prop up the branches or they would have been broken.

We ate all that we could, Mother gave them away to the neighbors, including the unpleasant ones, and she canned enough to last us all through the coming year. We had so many peaches that, in boy fashion, it was many years before I could really enjoy peaches again.

In a few months the neighbors moved. I do not mean to suggest that there is any connection here. But they did move; I am only reporting the facts. And that year, or the next, the tree died. That was the end of it — or the beginning.

The tree had never produced good fruit before; it never produced good fruit again: it did so just that one year. I know what some of you are thinking — the tree would have produced fruit even if Mother had not been so nice; it was something about the season or the chemicals. I don't know why it happened, I do not claim to. But I do know this, if she had returned evil for evil, it would not have happened for there would have been no tree, and a small boy would have missed one of the most beautiful experiences and one of the deepest lessons of his whole life.

Mother had an opportunity to get even and instead she sowed love, and there came forth a wonderful harvest. There was a harvest on the tree but there was also a harvest in her soul, in mine, in many others; a harvest which was abundant, that continues, and shall continue to the very farthest reaches of eternity.

Those of you who knew her saw some of that harvest in her face, and you heard some of it in her voice. You see, you are not beautiful when you are ninety unless you have lived long with the Lord. At ninety it is God's love, not cosmetics.

Do you have an arid place in your life? A patch of weeds, an old tree that will not bear fruit, an area of doubt, a plot of resentment, a get-even swamp? This is Mother's sermon. This is what she would say, "Sow God's love, and then step back and watch the miracle happen."

Mother died full of years and good Christian deeds at the age of ninety-one. I often wonder if her corner of heaven has a peach tree dressed in the full doxology of spring's glory or with limbs heavy with golden fulfillment.

10

Lillian Hitt

Lillian Hitt, wife of Eternity *magazine editor and author, Russell Hitt, had to decide what she would do with her free time. Would she give it to God, or would she use it for her own desires? Eventually every woman faces this decision. Lillian Hitt made a great discovery.*

I WAS A MEMBER of the little red chair set in Sunday school. I remember there were ten virgins on top of the blackboard. Though I didn't know what a virgin was, I knew five made it and five didn't."

Thus Lillian Hitt, orphaned at nine, recalls her earliest memories of the Plymouth Brethren Sunday school where she learned about God. A loving home with her aunt and grandparents supplemented her teaching, and at thirteen Lillian asked Jesus Christ to take over her life. But the story doesn't end there, as it hardly ever does. It is what has happened in between now and then, the stuff out of which life is made, that makes Lillian and her story what they are.

Today Lillian Hitt is well-known to women along Philadelphia's Main Line as the one whose excitement over the Bible first lifted their vision and introduced them to the reality of a personal God. The wife of author-editor Russell Hitt of *Eternity* magazine, the mother of two grown children, Lillian didn't always have this ministry. This story is how God zeroed in on her, won her obedience and gave her the gift of communicating His love.

Lillian Hitt had a flair for the business world. A warm personality, attractive, alert, she was a natural for success. Fresh out of high school, she entered the advertising firm owned by her grandmother's brother. (She still writes short feature articles for a Detroit agency.) Later, her membership in the Detroit Women's Advertising Club proved stimulating socially and professionally. Apart from working hours she taught a Sunday school class, and she wouldn't have admitted that life had any lacks . . . until the week the Women's Advertising Club sponsored a bridge and fashion show, which might have passed unnoticed in her church, except that a publicity picture showing Lillian holding bridge cards was published in the city paper. Her Sunday school class was suddenly taken away from her, and the reason related to the news clipping. Over a period of years there had been a slow, steady decline in Lillian's interest in spiritual things. Now this was the capstone, the finishing touch. She had had it!

"So, O.K. If that's what God is like . . ." and she heightened her quarrelsome relationship with Him, often accusing Him to release her own frustrations. It didn't happen all at once, but life was increasingly a maze of dead-end streets. Actually, the action taken by the church was a measure of love. Really good discipline always is. No longer did Lillian have a cloak to appease her conscience about her interest in God. She was out in the cold and knew it.

While Lillian chafed, God kept on loving. He is the Father who lets the son take his inheritance and go into a far country. He waits patiently, but let the son only begin to return and He rushes to meet him. He let Lillian see what life was like without Him, and then appeared so powerfully she had to make a choice.

In September 1938 Lillian sat in Moody Church in Chicago, her heart calloused by arguments. *Why, oh why,* she wondered, *had she ever let herself in for anything like this?* She turned off the droning voice of the preacher not long after he started speaking, and shut herself off from the congregation in the web of her own thoughts. But a higher, more persistent voice broke into her cell, and she began another dialog with God.

"If you want me back, why don't you have somebody whose preaching appeals to me?" she argued.

Just then the preacher's voice came through. He was reading Peter's words in Acts 10, "Not so, Lord." Incompatible words, the preacher said. You can say, "Not so," but it is contradictory to say "Not so, Lord." *Intriguing idea,* thought Lillian, and her quick mind recorded it as she fished in her purse for a pencil to write it down. She might try that on a Sunday school class sometime. Sort of catchy.

Then the preacher's voice again. "Now I want all of you to take out papers and pencils and write this phrase down. *Not so, Lord.* Cross out the word or the words you don't want there." If she hadn't already written the words, Lillian's stubbornness wouldn't have let her cooperate. But the words stared her in the face: *Not so, Lord.* She felt she was being confronted by God Himself and these words tore at her insides. The battle had been too long already, especially for someone who had met Him earlier in life. God bent her will to His. She picked up her pencil and crossed through *not so.* What a rush of relief! Before she had sought freedom, but found herself only a prisoner. Now she felt loosed, free. She knew she was reconciled to God.

The wanderer-back-in-the-fold now interested Russell Hitt, who had met Lillian seven years earlier. She had been going in the wrong direction when they first met, but he had not forgotten her. Never half-hearted about her enthusiasms, Lillian was now just the kind of wife Russ Hitt wanted.

After their marriage they lived in Chicago and Lillian kept

her career for a time. She transcribed two or three of Wilbur Smith's *Peloubets,* and worked for a Chicago advertising agency. She *liked* the business world. When their two children came, Lillian became a full-time mother and homemaker — a different kind of joy. But the children were soon off to school all day and Lillian was left with a hankering to return to business life. Her husband was away from home much of the time, and she missed the stimulation of a more active life. Employment enticed her, she had to admit it.

They had recently bought a home in a new development, and some well-meaning meddler had said, "When are you going to begin a Bible class in your neighborhood?" but Lillian had quickly shut out that suggestion. Her Sunday afternoon entertainment was reading the Want Ads of the Sunday *Tribune,* exploring the long listings under "Female Help."

This see-saw between the demands of the home and her love of employment went on for some time. One morning she decided the time had come for action. She would go job hunting. But before she went, she thought it might help to do her morning Bible reading. God's approval on her plans would be comforting. Her reading took her to Jeremiah 2 and the words of the 36th verse fell like a thud on her plans. "Why gaddest thou about so much to change thy way?"

Lillian had wanted a supernatural answer to her dilemma, and she got it. It was so devastatingly clear she couldn't even tell her husband right away. She waited until New Year's Eve to tell him (he hadn't thought job hunting was such a good idea anyway) that she had given in to God about a job.

God had something better in mind for her. Lillian laughs now about the appropriateness of the Jeremiah verse, and says, "God must have a wonderful sense of humor." But He got His point across and she knew a fresh submission to the One who is a better life-planner than she.

The idea of a neighborhood Bible class often returned to haunt her, but God knew she couldn't teach it. She was *sure* He must know that. She had told Him often enough. One night she dreamed that she was sitting on a sunporch, talking to a woman whom she had met only casually. She knew this woman was a Sunday school teacher, and she was saying to her, "Maybe you are the teacher for our neighborhood class." When she awoke and thought about the dream, Lillian got excited. And even more so when she attended a meeting and found the woman of her dreams sitting next to her. She had expected that recounting her dream would excite Mrs. Bendelow as it had her. But she was disappointingly casual about it. Mrs. Bendelow said she would talk it over with God.

While she was doing that, Lillian was doing some talking and thinking, too. Thursday would be the really only suitable day for such a class. She decided to ask Mrs. Bendelow for lunch, and then trying not to seem too overly eager, she asked, "If you did agree to teach, what day would it be?" Mrs. Bendelow listed off her commitments for the week and said Thursday was the only available day, and, yes, she would take the class. Lillian, who is really a Christian entrepeneur in the best sense of that word, gulped and went into action, going door to door to invite her neighbors to the class. And they came.

Lillian was still reading in Jeremiah, and the Word of God was coming to her with new application. The day the class began phrases from Jeremiah 31 fairly leaped from the pages, . . . *thy work shall be rewarded. . . . set thine heart toward the highway. . . . And they shall teach no more every man his neighbour, saying, Know the Lord: for they shall know me.* She knew she was entering into an adventure that was bigger than she.

Two weeks later she came to Jeremiah 48:11:

> Moab hath been at ease from his youth, and he hath settled on his lees, and hath not been emptied from vessel to vessel, neither hath he gone into captivity: therefore his taste remained in him, and his scent is not changed.

"It may have been out of context," says Lillian, "but God spoke to me about being at ease from my youth, and being unwilling to empty myself into the lives of other people. I thought, *I have a choice. I don't have to give what is in my vessel to anyone else. I don't have to be captivated by God. I could stay aloof.* But somehow I knew life would be as tasteless as this verse said it would be."

Reading on in the chapter she came to verse 27: *For since thou spakest of him, thou skippest for joy.* She chose that kind of life that day.

After Jeremiah comes Lamentations, and Lillian was struck afresh by the phrase in the second chapter, *those that faint for hunger at the top of every street* (vs. 19). The Bible was speaking to her situation, and she began to see people and needs and God's Word in a way she never had before.

Shortly after the neighborhood Bible class began, the Hitts visited friends at Lake Zurich, about thirty-five miles outside of Chicago. She told her friend there about Mrs. Bendelow and the class, and her friend lamented, "We have nothing like that here." Through Lillian's mind flashed the thought, *Wouldn't I like to teach a class here! Could I handle something like that, Lord?*

Not until a year later did the official invitation come. When it did, an eager Lillian drove a seventy-mile round trip to Lake Zurich and got her first taste of touching other women by sharing what God had taught her. It made her skip for joy, as God had told her it would.

"To make God real to others, He must first be real to you," Lillian says. "You cannot give away what you do not have. That's a principle of life. And those to whom you try to communicate will know whether your faith is fresh and contemporary, or some old-hat theory you picked up as a child and haven't used much since then. Suddenly God gave me fresh insights each day and then He let me share them. I have found out that the greatest adventure of all is living out the truth of God."

Just when things got really exciting, Russell Hitt accepted the offer to work with Donald Barnhouse, necessitating a move to Philadelphia. Lillian was picked up from two classes and set down in suburban Philadelphia on the Main

Line. After the drapes were up and the pictures hung, she found herself sitting in a house where the phone never rang, cut off from anyone she knew. She frankly felt left out and it went on so long she had a talk with God about it. *Lord, aren't you going to use me anymore? Am I on the shelf?* The Lord said *yes* to the first question, and *no* to the last.

Within a week a phone call came from a woman who said she had heard Lillian was a Bible teacher. They were planning a Christmas party for a class of colored children, and their missionary speaker couldn't come. Would Mrs. Hitt substitute? "A children's speaker? That scares me," said Lillian. "But the mothers will be there, too," said the caller. So Lillian accepted the invitation.

Out of this came her classes for colored women in West Philadelphia which continued for nine years. Shortly after Christmas that year she went to the first class and the lesson God gave her was about Philip and the eunuch. Lillian told the women, "Philip ran, so I come running. I come to join your chariot. Do you understand what you are reading? I run to join your group so we can learn together." No wonder they loved her.

About two years later Lillian Hitt met Martha Ayers, who also lived along the Main Line. Martha had recently faced up to the emptiness of her social life and was intrigued with Lillian's Bible classes in West Philadelphia. She thought, *I have the contacts. Why couldn't Lillian Hitt do this for Main Line women?* A notice in the paper said that Lillian was giving a devotional talk at a local church, and Martha went to hear her.

To Martha Ayers the simplest approach would be to invite her non-Christian and pseudo-Christian friends to a book review, so she asked Lillian, "Do you give book reviews?" But the book reviews never got off the ground. Instead Martha Ayers invited her friends to a Bible class and twenty-one women agreed to come that first morning.

Before Lillian drove over to the Ayers home for the class that day, she needed a word of encouragement from God on this project. God gave her the story of Deborah in Judges 4 from Dr. Ironside's *The Continual Burnt Offering*. She read, "Deborah . . . a faithful woman who knew God and dared to risk all upon His word . . . God delights to honor faith. He can be depended upon never to fail those who put their confidence in Him." Lillian said, *Thank you, Lord. I would love to be a Deborah for you in my generation.*

God took Lillian Hitt at her word and prospered the class. The class draws women from about twenty miles along the Main Line, from Cynwyd to Paoli, and anywhere from ten to seventy women meet each time. Other classes have come from this one. A couple's class has begun. Martha Ayers now teaches two groups of women, and other teachers have come alive in the group. Many of the women have brought unusual leadership back to their own church as a result of this teaching. For nine years now God has been inspiring lives through His Word, using the taught heart and lips of a woman who once told God she couldn't do it.

This Bible class gave a luncheon at the Philadelphia Country Club to which two hundred and fifty came in 1959 to hear Eugenia Price speak. A year later, they repeated the event with Henrietta Mears as the speaker. Billy Graham spoke to four hundred at a couple's brunch in 1961, and Governor Mark Hatfield was their speaker in 1965. More recently the Bible class sponsored a talk by Gertrude Behanna in the Bryn Mawr Presbyterian Church and seven hundred fifty heard the story of her conversion. These projects are a special outreach to which Bible class members invite their friends who may never have thought seriously about Jesus Christ. As I said, Lillian Hitt is an entrepeneur, and she has a big God.

Today Lillian is never without a new opportunity, but she weighs them carefully so that she can keep time for individual contacts. Recently she was invited to the Levittown Presbyterian Church to speak. She found a responsive, hungry group of women, eager for Bible study. "Come and give us a series of Bible classes in John's Gospel," they said. And so Lillian did, and her ministry has multiplied again through these women in the outlying areas of Philadelphia.

When Lillian Hitt told God she would like to share what was in her vessel, she had no idea of the long line of women God would bring into her life. One of these women who has been having psychiatric therapy said recently of Lillian's visits with her: "She comes and gives me Bible therapy."

Lillian Hitt knows something of answers to prayer, of sorrows, of dwelling between Ramah (the place of weeping) and Bethel (the house of God). But God is at work in *her* life, and it shows. Lillian has the shining look of a woman who is overflowing with good things to share. She has lived with the Scriptures and an afternoon with her can get you all excited about knowing God. Her strength in teaching is the devotional application of the Bible to everyday life. It is contemporary and relevant.

Along the Main Line it's not unusual to have a conversation like this. "How did you come to be so interested in the Bible?"

"I went to Lillian Hitt's class. Have you heard of her?"

It could have been so different. Lillian Hitt could have taken the easy way out. She had a choice. She didn't know she could do this, but she trusted God. "Once you've gone fishing," Lillian says today, "and have seen women respond to Jesus Christ, you cannot be content with anything less than outreach for Him."

II

Letha Scanzoni

Letha Scanzoni, wife of Sociology Professor John Scanzoni of Indiana University, has written two books for teenagers and writes a weekly column for The Sunday School Times. *As a girl trombonist, she wanted to be like Tommy Dorsey . . .*

TOMMY DORSEY IS MY IDOL! I wrote in red pencil beside the autographed sheet music I had just pasted into my scrapbook.

The famous trombonist and his band were the featured attraction of the Steel Pier ballroom that week of August, 1950. My family had just returned from an Atlantic City vacation, but my heart had remained behind along the boardwalk. In my day-dreams, I was still there — a sunburned, freckle-faced teenager standing right next to the stage, as close as I could stand without being struck by the slide of Mr. Dorsey's trombone! Oblivious to the dancing couples all around me, I stood there for three hours each evening, listening and observing.

"Someday," I vowed, "people will come to hear Letha Dawson and her dance band, too. I'm going to be just as good as Tommy Dorsey!"

At home once again in a small town nestled among Central Pennsylvania's scenic mountains, I took my trombone from its case and played the familiar Dorsey theme, "I'm Getting Sentimental Over You." In the two years I had been playing, I had already built up a reputation as a trombone soloist at school and community affairs. Now I would work harder than ever. No longer would it be two or three hours' daily practice, but double that. And it paid!

My junior and senior years of high school were a whirl of district and state talent contests, auditions, and solo engagements at almost every type of event, ranging from a Shriners' Grand Potentate's reception before thousands in formal dress to joining in homespun entertainment for small crowds at Sunday school picnics and country carnivals. When I traveled to a neighboring state to appear as guest soloist with a symphony orchestra, my joy soared into the stratosphere when I read the newspaper concert reviews which said: "Music critics have predicted outstanding success for the 15-year-old trombonist. . . . Orchestra officials said her musical tone is similar to that of Tommy Dorsey, noted band-leader."

I formed my own jazz band, "The Swing Teens," made up of teenagers from three different high schools. Our family living room virtually shook each week as an assortment of saxophones, trumpets, clarinets, drums — and even a washboard strummed on by our male vocalist — joined my trombone in blaring out Dixieland music and popular tunes. Customers at my father's adjoining service station must have wondered at the rollicking entertainment that came as an unexpected bonus while gas tanks were being filled and windshields wiped!

Fred Waring's Pennsylvanians appeared in concert at his hometown of Tyrone, Pennsylvania, and I was invited to a party in Mr. Waring's honor. He talked to me about my band, and I was thrilled. He told me how he had begun his musical career with a group of young instrumentalists rehearsing in his mother's parlor, too. His encouragement spurred me on to even greater determination to excel in popular music. How exciting can life get? Maybe I was already on my way to fame and fortune.

Surprisingly, underneath all the flurry there was within my heart a deep dissatisfaction. Weren't all my dreams coming true? What was this gnawing hunger for something more? Certainly I couldn't claim that life was empty or meaningless; I had my music, my goals and ambitions. Life had a purpose — a purpose most people commended. Maybe I just had the typical teen-age shakes!

I wondered sometimes if this wistfulness — this almost *painful* yearning — might not be a longing for God. I thought about Him a great deal while looking at the stars or walking alone through the woods or lying on my bed. I read the *Reader's Digest* condensation of *A Man Called Peter* and marveled that Peter Marshall could have such a personal relationship with God. Would it be possible for me to know God like that? There didn't seem to be anyone that I could ask about it who would really understand. And so, though carefully hidden under the surface, the search continued as my musical career progressed and high school graduation drew near. I auditioned at the Eastman School of Music in Rochester, New York, and was accepted for fall admission.

Sometime during that spring or summer, I was walking through a department store and noticed a table full of books under a sign marked "Clearance." I browsed for a few moments and was ready to pass on when the jacket and title of one book caught my eye. *That looks like a religious book!* I thought. Maybe it would have some answers for me. I gave the clerk fifty cents and left the store carrying a sale copy of Charles Sheldon's *In His Steps.* After reading it, my life would never be the same.

It was one thing to *read* about people whose lives were revolutionized by facing daily decisions with the question: "What would Jesus do?" It was quite another matter to apply it to myself. After all, the book was written in 1896. Surely, I reasoned, a teenager living more than half a century later couldn't be expected to take it too seriously or personally! But it was interesting religious fiction woven about a clever idea, and in spite of myself, I became involved. Especially did I find myself identifying with Rachel, whose commitment to Christ led her to abandon her aspirations to be a concert singer and instead to use her talents in rescue missions and social work. Near the end of the book a paragraph burned itself into my heart. It was to haunt me for weeks.

> The Bishop said that night, while Rachel was singing, that if the world of sinful, diseased, depraved, lost humanity could only have the gospel preached to it by consecrated prima donnas and professional tenors and altos and basses, he believed it would hasten the coming of the Kingdom quicker than any other one force. "Why, oh why," he cried in his heart, as he listened, "has the world's great treasure of song been so often held far from the poor because the personal possessor of voice or fingers, capable of stirring divinest melody, has so often regarded the gift as something with which to make money? Shall there be no martyrs among the gifted ones of the earth? Shall there be no giving of this great gift as well as of others?"

I blinked in astonishment. Those words slammed against all my self-centered ideas about what musical talent was for. I read the paragraph a second time, and a third. It seemed as though God were saying, "Why not you, Letha Dawson? Why not you?" I rejected that idea flatly — *that's asking too much!* I tried to go on with the story, hoping to forget such disturbing thoughts. I wanted to become absorbed once more in the story as a detached observer. But even when the book ended, I couldn't forget that paragraph.

During the following weeks I tried to analyze why it had affected me in such a way. Perhaps it was because the fictional Rachel was the first person I had ever come across who had given her music to Jesus Christ. I had never before heard of such a thing! But what did it have to do with me? *After all,* I rationalized, *I often played solos in many different churches.* Yet, could I say I was using my ability *for God?* No, I had to admit that I looked upon church engagements just as I looked on all other opportunities to play for an audience. I was interested in honors for myself, not God's glory.

I was getting an honest look at Letha Dawson's heart for the first time. I found an awful lot of "I" there.

Gradually, I began realizing that this whole matter went far deeper than my musical aspirations. It had to do with my *entire life!* But why was I, of all people, taking this so seriously? No one else seemed to. "It isn't as though I'm an irreligious person," I thought. Most Sunday mornings would find me in some church: it was the respectable thing to do in our town.

Yet, the Christianity I saw all around me was a very diluted form relegated to one hour a week — 11 A.M. Sunday, The rest of the week everyone lived as he pleased. On Sunday, one heard he should "Follow the Master's teachings." But what those teachings were and how they could be applied to life seemed matters of little concern. Surely this couldn't be the same Christianity as that of *In His Steps!*

When I was eleven years old I had "gone forward" at the annual revival services of a country church. The minister's wife had walked up the aisle with me and whispered, "Now you must ask the Lord to forgive your sins." I can remember voices all around me sliding through the gospel song, "Why Not Now?" People crowded around afterwards, crying and telling me I had taken a wonderful step.

But I'm not sure whether or not anything really happened in my heart that night. As young people neared their twelfth birthday, they were urged to do as I had done as a necessary preparation for church membership. My idea of "receiving Christ" seemed to be only some sort of transaction whereby one could be guaranteed eternal life in the hereafter. I had no conception of Christ's lordship over my daily life. No one had told me about that. Or it could be that my heart was rather thorn-infested soil, as in Christ's parable where "the cares of the world, and the delight in riches, and the desire for other things, enter in and choke the word, and it proves unfruitful" (Mark 4:19, RSV).

Remembering this incident in the little white church, however, provided false comfort during my teenage struggle. When I sensed the nearness of the seeking Shepherd, I'd quickly hide behind the memory of my going-forward-to-the-altar experience, reasoning that I had already "done that" and was on my way to heaven. It was a convenient excuse to dismiss the disturbing thoughts produced by reading *In His Steps.* I was like the sheep the Bible talks about, I was going my *own* way.

All efforts to banish the struggle failed. The novel's implications bothered me to such an extent that I began fearing I was losing my mind or becoming some sort of weird fanatic! One evening I went to my room determined to think the matter through, make a definite decision one way or the other, and get the whole thing settled. Flopped across my bed, I thought about my career ambitions for which I had worked and practiced so hard. I thought of all the people who had taken such an interest in me and provided so many opportunities for advancing my musical plans.

Turning over, I stared at the ceiling and considered all my dreams of money, my name in lights, the gay world of evening gowns and applause which I had already tasted. There came to mind a picture of my three fat scrapbooks filled with newspaper clippings about my engagements as trombone soloist and jazz band leader. And what about my relatives and friends? They had such high hopes for me. How disappointed they'd be if I were to turn about face suddenly and say I didn't care about these things any longer — that I wanted to invest my life in serving Jesus Christ! I knew people would say I had "gone crazy over religion."

No, the cost was too great. Maybe that hunger for God which started all this would go away if I were just to ignore it. *That's it! I'll forget all these absurd notions about surrendering my life to Christ,* I resolved. *After all, it's my life. What claim does He have to it?* I'd go ahead with my career plans just as everybody expected. Excitedly, I jumped up. Hurrah! What a relief to know the decision was made and the struggle over!

Almost without my realization, my hand reached toward a stand on which lay a New Testament, one the Gideons had distributed at high school. The pocket-size Testament flipped open to the twelfth chapter of John's gospel. Verse 43 virtually sprang out at me: "For they loved the praise of men more than the praise of God." I didn't know that was in the Bible! Now, like a perfectly aimed laser beam, it penetrated my innermost being. This was too much. I knew I was conquered; and like the fugitive of "The Hound of Heaven," I was stripped of my armor, beaten to my knees, waiting "love's uplifted stroke!" But strangely, this wasn't defeat at all. It was triumph! In surrendering I found the battle won instead of lost!

On my knees, I told God I wanted to be His completely. Since Jesus Christ had given His life for me, I wanted to give my life to Him. Everything — my entire being — was placed in His hands to do with as He chose. This included *music,* the "idol" which had almost been the cause of my saying *no* to Christ's "Follow me!" I found myself singing the refrain of "Living for Jesus." For the first time in my life I understood what those words meant. I was only a teen-ager, but I knew this was it — for life!

One of my earliest discoveries of this new life was that a surrendered life will be a guided life. It was hard to explain — even to some Christian friends — that one can really be *carefree* even about such crucial matters as career choice and life partner. But I knew God was leading step by step during those days at Eastman, and I simply wasn't concerned about that which worried so many others. God led me to some wonderful friends through Inter-Varsity Christian Fellowship and through serving on the musical staff of Rochester Youth For Christ. Both organizations were totally new to me, and for the first time in my life, I was with other young people who really loved Christ and wanted to live for Him.

One of the biggest thrills was seeing others come to know Christ, too. The summer before I entered Eastman, I had received a friendly letter from the girl the school assigned to be my "big sister." Most of the letter was an effervescent description of the social life I could have — plenty of dances, parties, and dates. I looked forward to meeting her with mixed emotions, wondering if we'd find anything in common now that I had such a changed outlook on life. Never would I have guessed that Carolyn was also a seeker, longing for God and not knowing where to find Him. Within a few months she personally trusted Jesus Christ, and there began for both of us wonderful times of spiritual growth as we shared God's Word, prayed together, led a dormitory Bible study, and on Sundays helped a young couple who had reopened a rural church. Today, Carolyn is a missionary to Japan.

One day I picked up an evangelical periodical and noticed an ad which said, "Has God called you to a ministry in music? There's no better place to study sacred music than Moody Bible Institute!" I felt God wanted me to transfer. My parents, who at first had been puzzled and a bit apprehensive about my being so religious, now accepted it and encouraged me as I considered this new step. My junior year began at M.B.I. instead of at Eastman.

At Moody, I was immediately asked to be trombone soloist on a gospel team. Again, this was an important part of God's plan — although I had no idea *how* important as the six-member group gathered together that first time and I was introduced to the speaker-leader, John Scanzoni! Each week, he would give me his sermon outline and I would arrange our musical program around the same theme to insure that the Chicago churches we visited each Sunday evening would receive double emphasis on the message.

Soon our interest in each other didn't stop at sermon outlines and musical programs. John and I were married the following summer and we continued to learn that God not only *guides,* but also *provides.* We arrived back from our honeymoon with about seventy-five cents in our pockets and no spare tire in the trunk (a blow-out in Canada had ruined the other tire). Our life became a series of amazements at God's love. He provided housing, employment, and every material need, even after Baby Stephen joined the family and John continued study at Wheaton College. Following this, we served for three years as home missionaries under Village Missions in Southern Oregon.

God puts desires in the hearts of those who trust Him. He gives ideas about the future — at least He did for us. Gradually it seemed right that John should continue his studies in sociology, aiming toward a Ph.D. This took a great deal of faith, and it wasn't an easy decision to make. Financially, the whole idea seemed fantastic. There were now two little boys to support, no prospects for employment, and almost no encouragement from friends as we contemplated graduate school.

But God is not limited by finite man's impossibilities. Three years at the University of Oregon again demonstrated that God is God. Why it takes people so long to realize this is difficult to understand. It was there, too, that the vision of reaching college students for Christ gripped us as never before. And it was there, in the lonely hours while my student-husband pored over books and research reports, that I began a ministry of writing — something John had urged me to do ever since the daily-letter days of our long separations during courtship. Articles for periodicals, music arrangements, and my first book, *Youth Looks at Love,* were written in a cramped, three-room apartment for married students. In between homemaking responsibilities and typing John's dissertation, I began a second book for teens, *Why Am I Here? Where Am I Going?* and a weekly column for *The Sunday School Times.*

Then came the cross-country move which brought us to Bloomington, Indiana where John is assistant professor of sociology at Indiana University. Here at one of the country's great centers of learning we face our challenge. Keen young students are looking for something to satisfy them. We believe Jesus Christ is the Cause for which they are looking, the Meaning for which they are searching.

When I think of the excitement of our encounters here with both faculty and students, of the opportunity of putting them in touch with God who is the Ultimate Reality, my self-centered dream of fame for Letha Dawson and her band seems the most hollow, inadequate idea I've ever had. I'm so grateful God broke through into my life and made it "bigger on the inside" than anything I could ever have planned for myself.

In these days of the "death of God" theology, I'm convinced He is very much alive. He has proven it so often in my life. One day, our kindergartener, David, seemed greatly disturbed when he overheard that John would be on a university panel scheduled to discuss, "Is God Dead?" His daddy assured him that God isn't dead; some people just *think* He is. David's reply was immediate and emphatic: "Well, they should look at the cross. They'd see He isn't there!"

Knowing that He isn't there any longer, but *here* — a risen Lord, active in today's world, active in my own life — has made such a difference! The university seems full of people asserting that modern man can find his own way — that he has no need for God. But some admit disillusionment with the wasteland of existence without Him. To them, as it did for me, the door to LIFE opens.

12

Dorothy James

God's fellowship is apt to take us considerably beyond ourselves. Dorothy James found herself doing a big job in a strange place.

THE DARK-HAIRED FELLOW who needed a haircut gulped down a too-generous swallow of coffee in his surprise, and it burned all the way down.

"You mean," he asked incredulously, "that you've spent five years in New Guinea living in a tribal village?"

The other students around the table in the Illini Union fingered the straws of their cokes, looking at Dorothy James with a new evaluation as she nodded *yes.*

"What in the world were you doing there?"

Dorothy James told them that she was a Wycliffe Bible translator, that she and another girl had lived in a Siane village, constructed an alphabet, compiled a dictionary in the Siane language, and then translated the Gospel of Mark for them to read. That was why she was now at the University of Illinois doing graduate work in linguistics.

They could scarcely believe her answer. Of all the places in the world, now made small and familiar by travel, New Guinea still has the most end-of-the-earth image to the average American. Dorothy didn't look at all like someone who should live in "the middle of New Guinea," they decided. She was entirely too feminine.

These outbursts of amazement over her mission have become familiar to Dorothy James. It's true. She doesn't look like the athletic-explorer type you might expect, and she isn't. She enjoys pretty clothes, concerts, good books and good company. She reacts like other women to bugs and snakes, and wilderness camping is not her first choice of vacation possibilities.

Dorothy's reasons for going to New Guinea are far more profound than these simple observations, however, and thereby hangs this tale.

"When I was a senior in high school, I heard for the first time that God took a personal interest in the details of my life from another high schooler," Dorothy reminisces. The high school music festival was approaching, and Dorothy was the accompanist for a young male soloist — a fellow who sat directly behind her in the school choir. At a practice session together, Dorothy was morose, and so he asked her with the tact of youth, "What's wrong with you?"

She told her sad story: the fellow she had been dating had suddenly dropped her like a cold fish, without giving any explanation. She was devastated.

"Don't take it so hard," the fellow said with an unusual gentleness. "That may be God's will for you."

Such an idea was shocking to Dorothy. What did God care about her dating life? That was her personal problem. The fellow was now in over his head, so he kept going. "Well," he said, "there's more to life than guys. Maybe God wants to show you that so you can turn to Him."

Either from confusion or anger, Dorothy didn't know how to cope with this idea. She stormed out of the room. He tried to catch her before she reached home, but she was faster than he, probably because she was so furious!

At the next practice he brought up the subject again. This time they were at her home, so she couldn't walk out. She did the next best thing. She burst into tears. Nothing could have frightened him more, but he kept talking. He explained how much God loved her, how much He wanted to give her purpose and stability. He told her the meaning of the death of Jesus Christ. And Dorothy stopped crying, listened and asked questions.

She had never understood any of this before, although she was brought up in a nominally Christian home. Her parents belonged to a church, but they didn't often attend. The minister's sermons were pleasant little homilies, and they could get that much at home. She had wondered about God, and had asked her mother once, "Is there really a God?" Her mother told her that of course there is a God and not to ask questions like that.

This fellow was answering questions she had wondered about for a long time. He told her how a person becomes a Christian, what it means to commit yourself to Jesus Christ. In short, he led Dorothy to a personal faith in Christ that night.

He had been afraid he had botched the job badly, but she had understood. He rushed back to his church to tell the other highschoolers attending a meeting there that Dorothy had become a Christian. The next day at school these Christian students gathered around her with excitement. The word spread. Her old gang were scared of her; her parents were horrified to hear her speak so dogmatically about her faith. But these Christian students accepted her into their fellowship and encouraged her growth in Bible study and prayer. Eventually her old friends regrouped, and Dorothy's senior year was unusually happy.

A genuine change took place in Dot James' life. Her family noticed it, as well as her friends. To Dorothy the biggest change was in her attitude toward the Bible. It had never made sense to her before, but now suddenly it came alive for her. God taught her what she needed to know as she read it. She has never doubted that the Bible was God's

Word because from the very beginning it has spoken to her with unusual clarity.

Dorothy went on to Illinois State University at Normal, where she became active in Inter-Varsity Christian Fellowship. Her first year glowed with a warm relationship with Jesus Christ. She introduced her roommate and another girl friend to Jesus Christ, as well as her sister.

She took advantage of every Inter-Varsity weekend conference she could attend to learn more about God. She learned how to lead a Bible study, went to the Urbana Missionary Convention, spent a month at Inter-Varsity's summer training camp in Canada (Campus in the Woods) and later spent three additional summers at Inter-Varsity camps.

This is the positive side of her Christian life during her college years, but all was not "sweetness and light." She often witnessed a disgusting amount of Dorothy and not much of God in her daily life. She came to hate the inconstancy that made her warm towards the Lord one time, cold and indifferent the next week. Her temper, her selfishness, her unwillingness to obey God, these problems died slowly. Her junior year she chalks off as an almost total loss as far as Christian growth is concerned, except for the fact that she came to see how meaningless life without obedience to Christ really is.

Though her life seemed to fluctuate badly, God was stabilizing her. Growth is only recognizable by a backward look of comparison. The summer before her senior year she enjoyed warm fellowship with the Lord Jesus and other Christians on campus and felt a surge of renewal. During her senior year God began to open her heart to the idea of missionary work. "That He ever saw potential in me," Dorothy marvels, "is just evidence of His loving grace."

Over and over God's Word was the means of keeping her on the track. She began to be concerned about the thousands around the world who did not have the Bible translated into their own language. She wondered how they could ever become mature Christians without it.

I remember one instance from the summer Dorothy

helped us at Cedar Campus. We were sitting on the porch of our cabin overlooking the lake. Dorothy came in with her Bible in her hand and shared what God had shown her during her Bible reading that morning. It was a fresh and stirring truth, and she was deeply affected by God's faithfulness in letting her understand this. With tears in her eyes, she said, "What if we didn't have God's Word to read!"

By this time Dorothy had graduated from college and was planning to teach school for a few years to pay off her college debt. When the debt was half paid, her father canceled the remainder. "Dorothy," he said, "you know what you want to do with your life. I want you to go ahead and do it." Both her mother and father have been a great source of spiritual strength to Dorothy in the adventures which followed.

The first step for missionary preparation was formal Bible training. Dorothy enrolled at Columbia Bible College in South Carolina. The college had a series of weekly foreign mission prayer bands, divided according to geographical areas of the world. Dorothy went first to the Southeast Asia group, but for some reason switched to the Pacific Islands prayer group.

Since then, Dorothy feels God in His wisdom prompted this change. One member of the prayer band was enthused about New Guinea. He was unusually well-informed about the island, and seemed to carry a heavy burden for the people of New Guinea. He had intended to go there as a missionary, but poor health would keep him at home. Sitting there in the meetings, listening to him pray for New Guinea, Dorothy absorbed his concern. She went in his stead.

Uncertain about mission boards, Dorothy attended the Summer Institute of Linguistics (SIL) in Oklahoma, a linguistic training program staffed by members of the Wycliffe Bible Translators. Here she learned how to decipher a spoken language, to identify sounds, to analyze grammatical structure. It was a fascinating summer. Her concern for New Guinea and her desire to do Bible translation dovetailed when she heard there were 500 tribes in the Australian half of New Guinea needing linguistic work. She was impressed by the spiritual leadership and scholarship of the Wycliffe people during her time in Oklahoma and decided to apply to Wycliffe for missionary service.

While at SIL, Dorothy met Ramona Lucht, and the girls developed a compatible friendship almost immediately. When it came time to fill out application papers, Dorothy put *First Choice*: *New Guinea,* under preference of place of service. Later, after she was accepted by Wycliffe, she requested Ramona as her translation partner.

Wycliff Bible Translators sends its prospective missionaries to a three-month Jungle Camp training to expose candidates to primitive life and the unexpected, as well as to demonstrate how a person can live in such a setting with reasonable comfort. "Jungle camp either develops your sense of humor or sends you home in a state of nervous collapse," Dorothy remarked. "If you panic over every snake or bug, this camp may change your mind about Wycliffe Bible Translators, and their mind about you!"

Finding a snake in her bed didn't seem so unusual after she had learned to build her own hut and make her own furniture. They made tables and beds out of round timbers by tying them together. The tying together proved to be the hard part. One girl's bed collapsed every night for four nights, until she learned to tie it together properly. Dorothy laughs as she recalls the night she and her partner invited two other girls from the next hut in for dinner. It was their first entertaining in Jungle Camp. Just as they sat down at the table to their elegant meal, cooked laboriously over an open fire, the table collapsed and the food spilled all over them. "At that moment," Dorothy said, "we had two choices, either to become upset or to laugh. We chose to laugh."

She couldn't laugh every time, but she was learning. The call of God to go to live among a people who had no written language was strong. If this is what you needed to do to obey this call, then Dorothy would do it and expect God not only to give her the grace, but enjoyment in it, as well. He has not disappointed her. She kept before her the goal of giving God's Word to a people who had never read it in their own language. She was reminded daily as she read her own Bible of this privilege.

As the ship pulled away from the dock the day Dorothy and Ramona sailed for New Guinea, they were glad they had said good-by to their parents in Missouri. That had been the really hard part about going. The first hours of their bus ride to the coast had been weepy enough. Now, seeing the ship leave the shore, conflicting emotions tore at them again. Scared, excited, sad, glad. . . . Leaving the homeland and its familiar culture was not easy, and they stood on deck, watching the shoreline recede for what seemed an endless amount of time.

The ship took them to Australia, where they spent three months helping to staff the Australian Summer Institute of Linguistics. "I had more difficulty adjusting to Australia," said Dorothy, "than I ever did to New Guinea. Perhaps it was because I expected the cultural shock in New Guinea, not in Australia. The fault was mine, not the Australians. They were gracious and hospitable, but I was insecure and homesick.

"Right off I did some things which I later found were culturally rude in Australia, and this only heightened my insecurity. I was afraid to open my mouth, afraid to act — for fear I'd be offensive as an ambassador for Christ. I was having to learn to trust the Lord all over again it seemed. Those first months were trying ones for me."

A midsummer Christmas with a picnic on the beach only made Dorothy's homesickness worse. (Strange how quickly things change. At home last Christmas, Dorothy was homesick for New Guinea!)

When Dorothy and Ramona arrived in New Guinea they were sent to another village to get tribal experience with a linguistic team of girls. This was a valuable learning time for Dot and Monie (as they call each other). They couldn't ask enough questions fast enough, storing all this information away for the day when they would be on their own in a tribe away from the civilized world. One of the things that impressed Dorothy the most was the love these two girls had for the people in their tribe. God has given this, Dorothy thought, and asked that He would do the same for her and Monie and that He would go before and prepare the way. She was discovering that even a strange tribe across the mountains in New Guinea was not frightening when God was in on it.

When the Dot-Monie team went out to the Siane tribe, their Wycliffe area director took them to the nearest town, hoping to install them in the government shelter (a grass house maintained for government personnel traveling through the area). They found a government officer, taking the census, installed in the house when they arrived.

This turned out to be God's "going before" because when the officer heard their plan, he took charge of the building of their house in the village. He spoke with the authority of the government, and not only got the Siane to build it quickly, but extremely well. It even had a leakproof roof! Dorothy and Ramona went back to the nearest town to wait until their home was finished.

Their village was about a hundred miles from the Wycliffe base camp, and the nearest town of any size was thirty-five miles away. The road to their village was passable during the dry season, impassable during much of the rainy season.

It was a great day for both the villagers and the translation team when the girls moved in. They hitched a ride to the village on a lumber truck going that way, piling on boxes and boxes of belongings and the pieces of woods which were the component parts of the furniture Monie had made while they had been waiting. The villagers all ran out to greet them and helped them bring their belongings into the house. Then they sat down on the floor and watched these strange looking girls set up housekeeping.

The girls didn't understand a word of Siane. The Siane didn't understand a word of English. There were no doors or windows, so those who didn't fit inside could gawk through an opening somewhere. Monie tried to organize the men to help put the furniture together by showing them which screws went where and how the pieces fit together. That turned out to be a hilarious experience, almost catastrophic for the furniture. Monie rescued some of it just in time. The men were about to pound in the screws they couldn't make fit!

Meanwhile the attempt at communication was pathetic. The villagers asked questions in Siane. The girls tried to understand with English replies, gesticulating madly. Monie did manage to get the men to put doors on the house, however, so they could lock themselves in at night. Dorothy caused a flurry for the rest of them when she made lunch.

There was no way to get the people out of their house except to leave themselves. When they headed for the village square, the people all trooped behind them. Seated in the square they began their first vocabulary lesson. They pointed to an object; the people said the word. Then the girls tried to repeat the word, which sent the Siane into fits of laughter. Dorothy pointed to the object and said the word in English. The Siane tried to say it, and it was the girls' turn to laugh. That first day they learned ten words and went back to their new home to record them. The vocabulary search had begun.

They did this each day for the first few weeks, trying to communicate on the simplest level in Siane. As soon as they were sure of a word, they recorded it in the dictionary they were compiling. They continued testing their vocabulary in a variety of contexts to make sure they had understood.

Meanwhile the business of living had to go on. One of the first problems came in the area of bartering. They were prepared to give salt, razor blades, matches or money in exchange for vegetables, firewood or water hauling, since they had to buy not only services from the people, but some food as well.

"What do you suppose is a fair price?" Dot asked Monie.

That was a good question; they decided they would have to feel out the answer. Dot suspected they were being tested to see if they would give more than was necessary. Not knowing how to behave in a strange culture is a nerve-racking affair. For the time there was no one to ask but the Lord. He sent a patrol officer through the village who was able to help the girls establish a fair price and communicate this to the villagers.

Each new day seemed full of these kinds of incidental crises, and they had to continually look to God for guidance. It took five or six months before they began to feel at home among the villagers and mutual trust was established.

The girls' house was made of woven bamboo. They cooked over an open fire, and used gas lanterns for light. An ingenious bucket shower kept them clean. Their beds were comfortable. What more could anyone ask? The girls got to work.

At the beginning, Dorothy's chief frustration was that she couldn't talk, and Dorothy likes to talk! When they had been in the tribe six or seven months, her desire to communicate something beyond the simplicities of daily life got the best of her. Kambe, an old woman of the tribe, had died. Visiting in the home after the burial ceremony, one of the women said to Dorothy, "Kambe knows Jesus now," thinking Dorothy would be interested in this.

She used the verb meaning *to be acquainted with* which Dorothy and Ramona had noted in their dictionary as a synonym for *know*. Encouraged by this word about Jesus, Dorothy said, "You don't have to wait until you die to *know* Jesus."

Immediately all conversation in the room stopped, and attention was turned on Dorothy. "You can know him now?" the old lady inquired. Dorothy assured her that she could.

"Do you know Him now?" they all inquired. "Do you know Him when you sing? When you eat? When you read from your book?"

Dorothy assured them that she and Ramona knew Jesus now.

Later Dorothy and Monie felt a mixture of elation and uneasiness about the conversation. That night they prayed that if they had not used the right words, God would show them very soon.

A few days later a young boy was sitting on the floor in their house looking through one of their *Time* magazines. He found a picture of Jesus and asked, "Is that Jesus?"

Dorothy replied, "It is a picture of Jesus."

"Did he see Jesus or did he just draw it?" the boy inquired.

Dorothy explained how no one living today has seen Jesus. This is just what they think He might look like.

The boy interrupted, "But you have seen Jesus!"

"Not with my eyes," said Dot, "but in my liver."

"But you said you *knew* Him the other night," the boy argued, and he used the verb *to be acquainted with* that Dorothy had used.

She had used the wrong verb. That was the reason for the unusual interest. The word she had used meant *to know because you have seen with your eyes.* The boy gave them another verb which meant *to know because you have believed or obeyed.* Dorothy made the dictionary correction and told the boy to go tell everyone who had been at the house that night that she had used the wrong word.

The boy spread the news through the village, and a barrier was crossed somehow in this experience. The villagers went out of their way to help the girls with difficult expressions and tried to say the same truth many ways to increase their understanding.

So the vocabulary and the dictionary grew. Sentence structure began to reveal a grammatical pattern. Again and again they tested words in context to see if they had grasped the right meaning.

"The Siane emotional words are usually in idiom," Dorothy explained. "We had to make sure that the words we chose for love, God, and other biblical concepts were not connected with taboos, sinful practices or sorcery. The best expression for love is an idiom which when translated literally means, *I hear you in my liver.* Try saying that to your dearest friend! Actually to the Siane this is an expression of deep appreciation and concern."

Dorothy found out the best idiom for hard thinking one day when Tela, their youngest language informant, said to her, "My ear is heating and heating until my head hurts." To think is *to heat in your ears.*

From the first, the girls were well received by the Siane. About the second month in the village, they were adopted into the clan system. One of the village women came as the spokesman with a group of others and, with difficulty, made Dorothy understand that she was her mother. "Your mother is far away," she said. "I will take care of you." From that point on, she always referred to herself as the girls' mother.

A white-haired patriarch of the village told them he would be their papa. His name is Ka. He knows three words in pidgin English, and one of them is papa. He proudly announces to every visitor to the village that he is the papa of these girls.

Ka is a spry old gentleman with a keen mind, a genuine extrovert. He has made up songs about Dot and Monie in which he tells how the girls need husbands, but they are far from home and there are no husbands here for them. The refrain declares the sadness of this situation. Dot has tape recordings of his singing, and they make her homesick for the village. Ka has also told the girls much of the ancient folklore of the tribe over the period of their five years there.

Only one problem caused them panic and seemed like Satan's psychological warfare against two single girls living in a remote village. It has been their hardest experience.

After the girls had been in the tribe about seven months, they began to notice holes in their woven bamboo walls. All anyone needed to do was to spread the bamboo to have a neat peephole. The first peephole was in the bedroom; the second in the shower room. The girls usually undressed in the dark, so the curious person couldn't see much, but still the holes were unsettling.

Then they began to hear someone pushing against their locked door each night after they put the lights out. No one ever broke in, but it was frightening and unnerving. The girls were well aware that their safety depended on God, but this door-pushing was a continual threat.

The crowning touch came one night when Dorothy heard a scratching on the wall near her bed and a voice whispered obscenities in pidgin English. The girls set a trap to catch whoever it was the next night. Ramona would wait near one of the windows with a flashlight after they had turned the lights off, and if the person came again, Dorothy would dash to the other window and they would catch him in the cross-beam of their lights. It happened again that night, but the culprit got away. However, the lights roused the whole village. Dorothy told some of the village women what was happening. They were very concerned and said, "Cut off his head with your big knife."

At the advice of their director, the girls hired villagers to build a fence around the back of their house where the bed-rooms were, and they had no trouble again for six months. Then one night when they had a girlfriend from base camp visiting them, they heard the pushing on the door again.

This time Dorothy took action in the village. She asked for all the village leaders, all the men, and anyone else who wanted to listen to come to the village square because she had some things to say. Then she explained that they had come to the village as sisters and daughters, and had been welcomed into the clans as such. She told what had happened and said that one does not push on the doors of their sisters and daughters. She said she knew it was only one crazy person in the village, but if it did not stop their director had said they would have to move to another village.

The villagers were sad at the thought of this, and whether they knew and punished the culprit, Dorothy doesn't know. But it never happened again. No one has ever broken into their house, even when they have been gone to base camp for long periods of time, and nothing has ever been stolen.

The girls' progress in deciphering the language and in translating the Scriptures was dependent on an informant who was willing to work. This was a major hurdle in the beginning. Just when they were making progress, the in-formant might decide he didn't want to work. Then God gave them two keen helpers.

Mbalo, a man approximately thirty years old, became their first-draft translation informant. He doesn't "know all the talk," as the people say, but he is keen mentally and willing to spend hours on a word or phrase to find just the right one for the verse they are working on. He will go to the Men's House and talk over a word with the older men who "know all the talk" and then bring the information back to the girls. Dorothy says he illustrates, demonstrates, acts out words — anything to help them understand. A heart condition keeps him from more strenuous work and he is glad to have this way to earn a living.

God has reached into the heart of Mbalo, and he now trusts Jesus Christ. Sometimes when he comes to work with Dorothy, she asks him to pray for both of them before they begin translating. Mbalo's prayers go something like this:

"Lord, you know this is hard work. It is too much for us. Clean us up from the inside out — our livers, our ears, our eyes. Clean us and straighten us so we can do your work straight."

"Beautiful words," Dorothy says, with shining eyes, because God's Word is revealing God's standards in Siane.

Tela, the younger informant, is a translation checker, and he has also been reached by God's Word. He is a fluent reader, and after Mbalo has worked through the first-draft with the girls, they check it with Tela. God has taught Tela's open heart many things through the Scriptures. When they were working on the Gospel of Mark, Tela said to Dorothy, "God is talking to us. He is saying you must not do this and this to my people. My people do this, I do this. We must stop."

When they did an abridgment of Genesis in Siane, Tela was struck by Genesis 24. He said, "Abraham's servant asked God to show him the right wife for Isaac and God did. I must ask Him to do that for me also."

In Tela the girls saw the first conviction of sin in the tribe. He began to be acutely conscious of wrongdoing. One day he came to see Dorothy and said, "I believe in Christ. I asked Him to clean me. I tell Him every night I want to be His. But each new day I am sinful by noon. How can I know if I am going to heaven?"

The girls quickly translated a few verses from I John for

him, and he was taught by the Word of God. He took these to share with the other villagers. Dorothy says, "You can't know how exciting this is unless you have also been the first one to give God's words to someone who has never heard them."

When Tela went to base camp with Dorothy and Ramona, he saw a film on the first-century church. He commented on the Roman dress of the characters in the film and asked Dorothy, "Did these people live a long time ago or do they live now?"

Dorothy told him how long ago it was.

Tela asked in amazement, "Did they have God's Book a long time ago?"

When Dorothy said they had, Tela looked very thoughtful. Then he said soberly, in the same way he had talked about his people's sin, "You have had God's Book for a long time. Is it not a sin for your people to keep it to yourselves so long a time?"

Dorothy thought it was. That is why she had come to New Guinea.

During their first term in New Guinea, Dorothy and Ramona completed the translation of a Genesis abridgment and the Christmas story, which they were able to circulate in printed form in the tribe a few months before leaving on their first furlough. Along with this, the people have typewritten pages of verses the girls had translated to teach some particular truth. About fifteen men in the village could read by the time the girls left.

Two weeks before they left, the Gospel of Mark in Siane came off the press, a prize accomplishment. This means the message of Jesus will be read, even though the girls have left the village. Mbalo began selling the Siane Gospel of Mark at government functions and in other villages, and for the first time some of the almost 17,000 Siane who live in New Guinea are hearing God's Book speak their own language. They have the message because two girls dared to trust God and go to a Siane village to learn the language and translate it.

It was with a good bit of emotion that the girls took a copy of Mark's Gospel to a Siane pastor who preaches to Siane in the highlands near the base camp. The four gospels in pidgin English had been his source for truth. Now as he read the Gospel of Mark in Siane, tears filled his eyes. He said, "Forgive me if I am slow to read. I have never read my own language before." Friends have written of the new fervor in this pastor's sermons and life now that he has God's Book that speaks his own language.

The girls are praying about their new translation projects when they return to New Guinea. They hope to give the Siane I John, James, possibly Acts and a synoptic gospel account. And always they must keep the dictionary up to date and take notes about new things they learn which will affect the revision of translation they have already done. They hope to begin teacher training classes so that the Siane can teach each other to read.

You can't know Dorothy James and feel sorry for her. While other girls have stayed home and fussed over their dresses hanging in neat rows in the closet, Dorothy has lived in a primitive culture where neat rows of dresses couldn't matter less. She has gone there in obedience to the call of Jesus Christ and in obeying she has been caught up in a redeeming work that will affect the eternal destiny of many who had never known before that God had spoken in a book.

When Dot James asked Christ to take over her life that night in her living room, she didn't know that He would lead her into this kind of an adventure, but she is not sorry. When she opens the Siane Gospel of Mark and reads its pages, she is moved with wonder that God would give her this privilege.

She has forgotten her scared human littleness, and has let God invade her life.

13

Eileen Guder

I wrote to Eileen Guder shortly after I had read her book, We're Never Alone, *and asked her if she would tell her story for this book. Neither of us knew at that time the details of the future she faced. Her chapter bears the mark of a pilgrimage through sorrow, for she wrote it just a few weeks after the death of her husband from leukemia.*

As A VERY LITTLE GIRL when the real world around me was unsatisfactory, I created an imaginary one more to my liking. I used to play in a vacant lot full of weeds, but I saw it as a fairyland of lawns and flowing streams and trees, and I put a little girl there as a playmate and named her Bluebell. We had a marvelous time — Bluebell and I. It was a fake world, but it was a good one.

Some people think of Christianity like this — as largely a matter of the imagination. Just wishful thinking. Peace, joy, heaven — all the good things Christians talk about are just drummed up products of an active imagination. But I have spent a good part of my life proving that this is not so. The proof has come as a result of a sometimes painful search, but today as a Christian I know and experience realities unknown to me before.

As I said, the color in my life while I grew up was inside of my mind. The outside world was drab enough during the depression. Since I did a great deal of reading, my views of life were in some areas quite mature, formed by better minds than mine, but in practical matters of living I was very naive.

Russell Guder, whom I fell in love with at eighteen and married at nineteen (he was an ancient twenty-two) was a nominal Christian when we married. I had been raised in a small, fundamental church and had made a commitment to Christ, but the life and vitality of the Gospel seemed very far removed from the boredom I felt with the church.

Russ and I agreed on one thing — we turned our backs on the church. We may not have known what we wanted, but we knew what we did not want — to live careful, neat lives which conformed to a careful, neat group. We did not renounce our faith, or anything dramatic like that, but we simply removed ourselves from Christians.

After seven years of marriage and three children, a hitch in the Navy during the war for Russ, we were both vaguely dissatisfied with life. Where was all the fulfillment I had looked for? Occasionally I wondered what God was about, letting everything get in such a mess. If I prayed it was when something threatened to disturb our little lives, or I became anxious. My attitude toward prayer was like that of a nervous plane passenger reading the instructions for emergency landing: "But I do hope it won't come to that."

We moved to Los Angeles after the end of World War II, still restless and looking for something. We knew we had found it when we attended the Homebuilders Class of the First Presbyterian Church of Hollywood. These young couples were *different*. They weren't pious, or dull, or imbued with the saccharine spirituality we had feared, but vital and intelligent — and something more. We wanted what they had. It was as simple as that.

Some people meet Christ for the first time in a sort of blinding revelation. We met him, and knew that He had been the One we had met and ignored a long time ago. Looking for color and depth to life, we had been wading in the shallows of mediocre living when the ocean of His life had been there all the time. We began to read, to study, to make new friends, and a most marvelous thing happened. In giving ourselves completely to something other than our own concerns — to Christ — it became clear that we were delivered out of a total and deadly absorption in our own selves, an absorption which had effectively sealed us off from any real relationship with others. It is embarrassing to have to make this admission, but to be honest I must admit that all my shyness, insecurity and inadequacy had been due to having been centered on one thing — me.

That was one of the great liberating moments of my life. But the liberation was not finished, by any means. I had to learn again and again and in new and sometimes painful ways that I was not the center of the universe. To know Jesus Christ was to know that He loved me; but He also loved others, and if He was concerned about them then so must I be. But that was only the beginning of a new road, a road with many rough places ahead.

You often hear testimonies to the effect that all problems were solved when Christ came into one's life, or glowing reports of financial crises averted, miraculous recoveries from illness, and even the most minute daily irritations gone. Russ and I heard such testimonies and we looked eagerly for the same wonderful smoothing away of difficulties in our lives. But quite the contrary took place. Not only did we still struggle under the same old financial burden, but a series of new disasters came along. Russ had an unexpected emergency surgery. In 1948, while we were at a Christian Conference for young married couples our two youngest children, Carole Ann and Donna, became ill and after a few frantic days it was apparent they had polio. Darrell, our son, was nearly nine at the time, Carole Ann was seven and Donna was four. Donna had very little involvement, but Carole Ann's right leg and her stomach muscles were weak, and after three months in the hospital there was a year of out-patient treatment for her.

My life was lived on two levels during those years. One part of me kept on with the business of being a wife and mother, enjoyed my friends, went to Bible study groups and even thought and prayed about God and His purpose. But beneath that surface life lay the questions and fears that had accumulated, sometimes fearfully shaped and colored by my imagination. God might love me, but what was His purpose for my life? It might not be what I wanted at all. So far His purpose seemed to involve us in nothing but difficulties, and yet we kept hearing so many happy testimonies from others who apparently floated through life. What was wrong?

I began to examine myself nervously, probing to see if there was some lack of faith that lay at the bottom of all this trouble. I remembered my old make-believe fairyland in the vacant lot, and sometimes wondered if I was doing the same thing — trying to imagine the weeds and dry earth of reality into the green lawns and clear rivers of the Gospel story. Eventually I said, like Peter, "Lord, who else should I go to? Your words have the ring of eternal life." And yet the unresolved questions of trouble, pain and seemingly unanswered prayer still lay under the surface.

In 1950 in the fall, Carole Ann developed some alarming symptoms and after months of anxiety and turmoil we knew she had a brain tumor. During that time when the diagnosis was in doubt I must admit that my interior life was the real one. While I went about my daily duties mechanically, I was waging a bitter battle with God. Why, after years of one small disaster after another, should this final blow be added? I refused to accept it. God had become an enemy, bent on snatching everything away that made life good. I read the Bible and it was dead words except for one passage which might have been my own: "When I looked for good, then evil came unto me; and when I waited for light, there came darkness" (Job 30:26).

Carole Ann's tumor proved to be inoperable, and after surgery she lived for two weeks in a coma, then died. Russ and I had finally come to an exhausted acceptance of her death. If this was God's will, the battle was over. But the scars remained. To simply give in because there was nothing else to do was not good enough, not good enough to live by. Our whole Christian philosophy had to be re-thought. It took years and it was slow and painful. Out of that, however, came an eventual serenity based not on wishful thinking — not on our imagination painting hopeful but impossible pictures — but on the solid rock of Biblical truth.

We began to examine the presuppositions of our faith and tested them in the light of the Bible. We found a far different view of life. The Bible does not promise, nor did Jesus ever promise an easy path through life, a shallow happiness, or any kind of success. The key-word of Jesus' last message to His disciples seemed to be in the words, "You will find trouble in the world, but never lose heart, I have conquered the world!" Not escape from the common ills of mankind, but strength to go through them, and a Companion who has been there before. More than that, an eternity with Christ. Not a temporary stalemate, putting off death which must come to all of us, but a real victory over death. The conclusion we came to has never altered. It is simply this: that Christ died for our sins not to spare us the sorrows of this life but to go with us through them, and to bring us at last to be with Himself.

The years since then have been for the most part full of unexpected blessings. Darrell and Donna have been infinitely rewarding, and their friends filled the house. Darrell, after two years of college here, finished his education in Hamburg, Germany, receiving a Doctorate in Philosophy there in July of 1964. There were some trips to Europe for Russ and me, along with Darrell and Donna, an undreamed of thing for two young depression kids twenty years ago. Darrell married a young woman whose family we had known, a completely joyful event for all of us. I began to write the book, *We're Never Alone,* although in somewhat desultory fashion and with fear and trembling. Sometimes Russ and I would talk about our life together, and the unexpected turns it had taken. We always ended up by thanking God for a wisdom and goodness higher than we could have asked for.

In March of 1965 Darrell came home only long enough to be ordained a Presbyterian minister in our own church. Then he and Linda went back to Hamburg to work for three years there in youth work. It was one of those times in life when we seemed to stand on a high peak with all the clouds below, and very close to heaven. Donna was planning to be married the following December, and Russ and I felt that we had been able to finish the most important responsibility ever given to human beings — that of starting one's children out in the right direction. We were deeply thankful.

All year Russ seemed to be tired. We thought it was because of the heavy load of responsibility he carried in business. He had his own C.P.A. practice, and the work grew increasingly heavy. Finally, in October of 1965, he was so weary that he went into the hospital. After some weeks of uncertainty a diagnosis of leukemia was made. The prognosis was not good — three to six months usually, in such cases.

That first night I spent alone after receiving the news, while Russ was in the hospital, was the worst. My incorrigible imagination painted the whole lonely future in dark colors for me; and yet, there was the one thing that made the difference. I knew that God was in control. There was none of the fierce rebellion I had felt at Carole Ann's death. That issue was settled. Russ faced the future with unbounded trust in God and his strength sustained me.

Donna was married on the 18th of December and Russ took her down the aisle. He had gone through a very low period, and I know the doctor wondered whether he'd make it, but he had asked God for this one thing — and he did it. Darrell and Linda had come home for the wedding and Christmas, and that holiday season was a time illumined by the joy which God alone gives. It has nothing to do with circumstances but is, I believe, a very faint foreshadowing of that unfading glory which will be ours in eternity.

Russ read and meditated and prayed, and enjoyed visitors. We did all we could not to live a "sick" life. Leukemia is an ugly disease, and the enormous quantities of medicine he took, the visits to the doctor and the times spent in the hospital could have crushed us both. We were determined, however, not to let those things set the tone of whatever time there was left, and the last weeks were good ones. Russ was a man of quiet courage and I know there was much pain that he never mentioned. The end came quickly, so quickly that his last conscious moments were spent at home instead of in a hospital. There were so many things to thank God for.

Now he is gone and I still feel somewhat frozen. The inevitable time of adjustment to a new kind of life has come, and a kind of recollection and evaluation of the past goes on. My dominant emotion is one of gratitude for all the *good* Russ and I knew together. Our children are a source of deep delight. We have been blessed with friendships which have strengthened and helped us both. There were the trips we were able to take, the real enjoyment Russ got out of his business, the satisfactions of home and church. We had twenty-seven years together, not always placid, but the marvelous thing about a growing relationship with Christ is that His grace seems to spill over backwards, as it were, so that even the troubles of the past are transformed.

Even during Russ's illness there were new blessings. When he first became ill we were introduced, by letter, to Eugenia Price whose books we had read and loved. Floyd Thatcher was the "mutual friend," and the letters that came from Genie to Russ and me were always an infusion of new life — warm and encouraging and electrifying, all at once, a source of strength to us both.

What about the future? It is safe in the hands of the One who brought me safely through the past, and who keeps me now. There will no doubt be some problems; there always are. I will doubtless hurt inside; I do right now. But there will be the warmth of dear friends, work to do, laughter and tears each in their measure.

I could never have imagined the past twenty-seven years in all their richness and reward, however vivid my imagination was. An imagination is a wonderful thing to have. It can add color and life; it can paint pictures and build castles. But I have learned one thing above all else, that the reality that is ours in Christ is beyond and above any of our imaginings. I have no desire to turn inside to a world of make believe. Knowing Jesus Christ, I expect Him to help me look my today and my tomorrows squarely in the eye, and find Him sufficient.

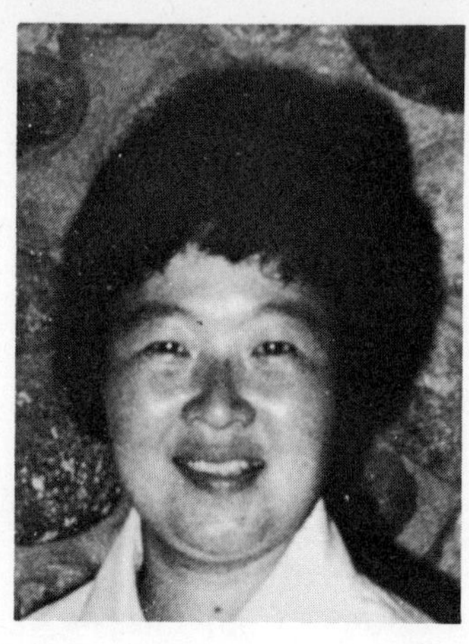

14
Yoshiko Taguchi

Yoshiko Taguchi is a survivor of Hiroshima. She was sitting at her school room desk, a half a mile from the center of the blast, the morning the bomb fell. Her story contains two miracles, for she not only escaped with her life, but she found New Life out of the sorrow of Hiroshima.

HIROSHIMA was a dark day in the history of the world. Before August 6, 1945, Hiroshima was known in geography books as a large, industrial Japanese city. Today it is a reminder of the awful dilemma of mankind. For on that fateful day the first atomic bomb was dropped, an estimated 70,000 persons died and another 70,000 were severely injured by the blast. How many died later of the effects of atomic radiation is unknown.

The moral implications of Hiroshima have been widely discussed; books have been written about the decision to drop the bomb and about the effects of the blast. Today's school children somewhat unemotionally read the facts as history.

But Hiroshima was more than a tragic blot on the pages of history books. Hiroshima was people. Men, women, school children, fathers, mothers and infants. And God, the omnicompetent One, saw and reached down through death and terror with His touch of redemption.

Fifteen-year-old Yoshiko Taguchi almost missed her part in "Hiroshima" that day. Her four-year-old sister was sick and her mother had wanted her to stay at home and help. Yoshikosan (as her close friends call her) left the house early, annoyed with her feelings of guilt. As a high school girl, which was her first duty? To stay at home and baby-sit, or help Japan in her life-and-death struggle against the United States? Two loyalties conflicted.

Such unhappy changes had been brought about in her life by the war! Her father had moved the family away from the bombing raids in Tokyo to Kakagawa, about fourteen miles from Hiroshima. Her parents had decided that the best high school for her older sister, who was then a senior, was the Methodist high school in Hiroshima. Early each morning Yoshikosan went by train with her sister Kimikosan to this same school.

Yoshikosan didn't like the school and she never would, she decided. She resented going to a school with Christian teachers. Call it prejudice, if you like, but their ways simply were not Japanese. They had been influenced by foreigners. She especially hated it when the Christians prayed in the school. They had no altars and no visible gods to pray to, and each time she had to put her hands to her face to suppress the giggle she felt coming at such ridiculous hokus-pokus. The hymns were nice, and she often caught herself humming or singing the words to herself.

When they told about Jesus, Yoshikosan felt her resentment heighten. Jesus was the Western man's idea of God. "Suppose he did live," she would scoff to her friends. "That was two thousand years ago. Even if he did heal the blind and raise the dead, that was still two thousand years ago."

Every Japanese was involved in war work on some level. Yoshikosan attended school and also worked for the government-operated railroad offices located in the high school in Hiroshima. Leaving often at 5:30 a.m. and returning at 7 p.m., she put in long days to do what she could for the Emperor. She felt tired now as she rode the crowded train into the city. At the station in Hiroshima she collided with a girl friend in the surging mobs, and they chattered on for a few minutes about their plans to meet for lunch at noon. Then Yoshikosan hurried on to the school. It was an ordinary day.

At 8:15 that morning Yoshikosan finished adding a long column of figures in the accounting office. Just as she was about to turn the page, her world blew apart. A shattering explosion — unlike anything imaginable — threw her across the room. The building rocked, then collapsed from the tremendous concussion. The noise! It sounded as if the world were ending. The pressure, the vacuum, the hot air, the debris in the air — dazed, Yoshikosan found herself lying in a mass of blood, broken glass and plaster, a heavy beam pinning her legs to the floor.

Shouts of confusion, panic, and cries for help came from outside. Footsteps ran past the building. Yoshikosan struggled to free herself, only to fall back into the debris again. She knew with an awful fear that unless she got out soon, she would die in the wreckage. Shouts of "Fire! Fire is coming!" revived her. She tried again and again, determining to pull hard enough to lift the beam and free her legs. Finally, by a strange combination of miracle and effort, she was free! Her legs were swollen and bleeding. Scared, bleeding and weeping, she crawled through the rubble to freedom. Once outside the building, she collapsed on the school grounds.

Again she was roused to consciousness by cries of "Fire!" People ran past, screaming and crying. Terror has an awful sound. Yoshikosan called to the passers, "Someone please help me," but most ears heard only their own private fears. Somebody finally did stop to help — a school friend who didn't even recognize Yoshikosan in her disheveled, plaster-caked condition. She helped her to her feet, and together they hobbled away from the burning school. Three hundred and twenty students and eighteen teachers died that day in the school, one half mile from the center of the blast.

That night Yoshikosan huddled with the sick, the dying and the terrified mob along a river on the edge of the city. It was an unforgettable night. The morning, beautiful and hot, revealed the horror of all that had happened, the sickening condition of the half-alive, the city in wastes, and all the backwashes of debilitating fear. American planes flew overhead to survey the damage. Rumors raced through the crowds. Certainly one thing was obvious: this was an explosion unlike any that had ever happened before, and the Americans had done it.

But Yoshikosan was alive, and she must get word to her family. So, with her clothing in tatters, barefooted and bloody from hundreds of cuts, she started to walk and crawl towards home, fourteen miles away. At the edge of the city she was able to get the last train out of Hiroshima which brought her within a few miles of her home.

Yoshikosan's mother had been meeting every train with food and clothing, hoping against hope to find her daughter among the fleeing survivors. When at last Yoshikosan staggered off the train, her mother tried to clean her wounded child — no one could enter a clean Japanese home looking like that, even after an atomic blast. Cleaning up wasn't easy, for Yoshikosan had severe cuts and the force of the blast had driven glass and dirt into her skin. And food made her vomit. It was then the mother knew that her daughter was not just injured; she had a strange sickness.

Days later the war was over, but what good was that? Yoshikosan's nose bled, her hair began to fall out. She had a continual fever. Other refugees retched in the streets, and talked about the radiation from the bomb which was causing even the survivors to die. Yoshikosan's mother covered her with wet cloths to assuage the fever. It took a week to find a nurse who would come and dig out the glass from her cuts. Infection had set in by then. The nurse probed and pried, as Yoshikosan gritted her teeth, too weak to do more, and thirty-six pieces of glass came out of smelly, festered wounds.

Radiation sickness is a horrible thing. Yoshikosan was hemorrhaging internally and knew she was dying. When it seemed unbearable, she would vacillate between wishing she could die and terror that she might. She remembers screaming out during these times, "Somebody help me!" But no one knew anything more to do. Her mother became ill from the strenuous rigors of taking care of Yoshikosan day and night, week after week. As she tried to comfort her daughter's fear of death, Yoshikosan thought maybe if her mother would die too, they could take the long journey together and she wouldn't be so afraid.

One day when the fear of death was particularly acute, a hymn she had sung at the Christian school came to her mind. She didn't know the words were from the Bible, but her lips formed the words,

> God is our refuge,
> Our refuge and our strength
> In trouble, in trouble, a very present help.

If Jesus is a dead god, having lived two thousand years ago, Yoshikosan wondered, *why did the Christians use the words "a very present help"? Maybe this One who lived two thousand years ago and healed the sick was a living God, just as the Japanese Christian teachers had said. What if this was the truth? And the message about Him had come from the West . . . and so had the plane that dropped the bomb . . .* Yoshikosan's troubled thoughts ran on. *Could this God* hear *my cry? Could He* save *me? Could He* heal *me?* Hear, save, heal . . . *if He were a living God he could.*

She didn't know how to pray like the Christians did. She had bowed before the family god shelf daily ever since she could remember, but that was not praying. Out of desperation she breathed a prayer for help, remembering to add "in the name of Jesus" as the Christians did.

Yoshikosan says she knows God heard that prayer. A peace came over her instantaneously; the fear was gone. She knew He had heard and that He cared about her. She had contacted the living God, without realizing that He had been there all the time waiting for her to acknowledge Him.

Slowly her wounds began to heal, the hemorrhaging stopped; the vomiting, the nausea were gone. All around others continued to die, but in two months' time Yoshikosan was healed. She knew Jesus had healed her, and never lost the sense of wonder at what had happened when she prayed that first time. Now that she was well she knew she must serve Him and find out more about Him, and she set about to do just that.

One by one she began convincing her family that Jesus was a *living* God who heard prayers. Japanese families don't change their beliefs easily, but Yoshikosan was living proof of His reality. Her older sister believed first. Her father, an electrical engineer who had been away on a business trip when the bomb fell, told Yoshikosan that he had been observing Christians for years and had been impressed with their humility and peace. He came to believe in Christ.

Yoshikosan's witness was genuine, and one by one others in her family came to trust Christ. Her mother held out the longest. She did not commit herself to the truth of the Christian message until her father died. Stricken by the thought of eternal separation from her family, the mother saw no reason to go on living. Yoshikosan and Kimikosan helped her to trust Christ for herself that night.

In 1949, when the war was long past, Yoshikosan graduated from college and began to work with missionaries who had now returned to Japan. When one missionary returned to the States because of tuberculosis, she met two others who needed her help. Her knowledge of God's Word grew, but it wasn't enough to satisfy her. She saw on every hand the need for Christian leadership in her country, and began to pray that God would lead her to a school where she could study the Bible for herself.

Her missionary friends arranged for Yoshikosan to study in the States, and in 1959 she arrived in Seattle for schooling at King's Garden School. Throughout her years in America she tried to discover what her place might be when she returned to Japan. How could she best reach her own people?

What should she do with her training when she returned? Increasingly, God spoke to her about university students as the key to reaching Japan. In 1963 she returned to Japan to join the staff of the Japanese student movement — Kirisutosha-Gakusei-Kai — the Japanese equivalent of Inter-Varsity Christian Fellowship in the States. The KGK is thoroughly Japanese — sponsored, planned and paid for by Japanese Christians — and designed to encourage Christian leadership.

The KGK has not had many women staff workers. While many women attend the university in this education-conscious country, still the role of a traveling woman staff worker requires a bit of extra courage. And Yoshikosan has this. Open-faced, forthright, she initiates friendships, has an irrepressible giggle, is full of new ideas, and is perfectly charming. The university girls in a changing Japanese society love her and are attracted to Jesus Christ through her. One old-time missionary of some forty years in Japan grumbled to us that she was "terribly American . . . not at all a proper type Japanese girl." But God has transformed Yoshikosan into a proper type *Christian* girl with a radiance that is supra-cultural.

We met Yoshikosan first as a student in the States, and later visited her in Japan where she was doing student work. She was our guide on an excursion to the resort area of Nikko, even packing a lunch for us to eat on the train as we journeyed north. However, after she had hard-boiled eggs for our lunch and set them aside to cool, she picked up unboiled ones and put them in the lunch bag. Having discovered our lunch in the somewhat slippery condition of broken raw eggs, Yoshikosan put her hands over the lower part of her face, as Japanese girls are wont to do, and giggled periodically the rest of our tour. Everything we did with her turned out to be an adventure!

Yoshikosan knows how to laugh at herself and has a natural bouyancy that fits her especially for the great demands and discouragement of her work for God in Japan. She has met God in Christ and *knows* it. Her enthusiasm for Him gives irrefutable evidence of His reality as she confronts Japanese intellectuals with His claims.

Yoshiko Taguchi is a beautiful example of the grace of God. Who but God can reach down into so horrible a situation as Hiroshima and make good come out of it? No wonder one of His names is Redeemer.

15

Antoinette Johnson

"Toni certainly has changed!" her friends comment at quiet dinners and cocktail parties in the social world of Palm Beach. Most of them know why. More than Antoinette Johnson's regal bearing and attractive warm personality is evident when you are with her. There is a radiance about her, as if she knows a wonderful secret. She is not hesitant to talk about it, even though people don't always understand. For her secret is a Person who has changed her life.

A FAILURE AT FOURTEEN! I smile now as I reflect on my agony over myself, especially when I looked in the mirror. Horn-rimmed specs, braces on my teeth, already taller than any of the other girls — what an assortment of deficiencies to drive a lonely young girl to despair.

I might have taken these rather typical teen-age phenomena in stride had a divorce not destroyed the security of our family life. When my parents decided their marriage was unbearable, I was not really surprised because their unhappiness had been evident for years. Children are more perceptive than their elders think. I knew, for instance, that I could probably never please my beautiful, demanding mother, who only made me feel more like an ugly duckling. I sensed that my real support in life would always come from my father. It was Father who taught me to walk and take advantage of my five foot ten and a half inches height. "Toni," he'd say, "walk like a queen. People seldom notice the mistakes of a short person. But you're tall. You'll be noticed."

Our home was cushioned by wealth. Thirteen servants catered to our needs, including chauffeurs for both Mother and Father. I attended a private day school in New York and loved learning and the discipline of achieving. I had everything I needed.

When my parents divorced, I was attending a fashionable boarding school in Aiken, South Carolina. My enthusiasm over being "on my own" soon turned to ashes. My classmates challenged every standard I had cherished. I was innocent, naive. Scholarship was not admired by these students, nor was discipline, nor good conduct, nor high morals. I didn't attract boys and I was teacher's pet. That combination finished me. I was not a success by the girls standards. I was a failure in the world at fourteen — angular, awkward and lonely.

During this time of terrible loneliness God convinced me of Himself. I had been brought up in the front pew of an Episcopal Church in New York. Father was a vestryman and we were often in church. When my brother and I were small, Mother read Bible stories to us. But it was Mother's personal maid who best reflected God's love in my childhood. Much like the Hebrew maid in Naaman's house, she made God real to me. I didn't know much, but I knew Jesus loved me and had died for my sins. I remember now leaving the other girls and going off by myself with my prayer book to seek His friendship. I loved God with all my heart.

I asked for baptism and confirmation in the Episcopal Church, but teaching was confined to communion and one service on Sunday. Somewhere I had heard that I should do everything for the glory of God and I liked that thought. It appealed to my idealistic bent, so I adopted that as a rule for my life. How little I really knew about the standards of His glory I was only to discover later.

I never questioned the pattern of life in which I grew up. Young women in my society went to finishing school, made their debut, and were married. I did the same. At twenty-two, in love with the idea of marriage, I married the first acceptable man who asked me. He was as immature as I. We played at life, both selfish and spoiled. After two and a half years and a lovely baby girl, we divorced. I adored my Father, a rock of stability in all my distresses, and I went to Palm Beach to be near him. Dabbling in real estate, I was now successful as a young divorcee — an acceptable role in the right circles.

I married again. This time to a big industrialist twenty years my senior. It looked good this time, stable and socially prominent. In retrospect I think that I was trusting a father image, but I was overwhelmingly disappointed. This marriage lasted nearly ten years, and to it was born our wonderful son. I had everything but happiness, and not even wealth can assure that.

After a three-year interval, I tried again. Husband number three turned out to be a tragedy. During two and a half years of this marriage, I lived with death. The appalling depravity of his life left me bewildered. And while it seems strange, during each of these marriages I attempted in my ignorant way to carry out my life motto — to do all for the glory of God. How did you help a wretched man like this, I wondered. In an attempt to do this, I underwent psychoanalysis with him. So terrifying was life with this man, I felt the only safe two hours of the day were spent in the doctor's office.

My husband forbade my going to church, and I am sure that the only thing which kept me sane was my habit of holding onto God. I remember one day with amusement, however. The psychiatrist was pussy-footing around about a father complex. I blurted out, "Are you perhaps considering a father complex on my part?"

He responded with the nebulous nothing of indirect counseling.

I said, "If you had known my father, you would have one, too. And my heavenly Father goes beyond even that." I'm still learning the magnitude of truth in that last statement.

After this fiasco, I became increasingly active in the church. I volunteered to teach a class of difficult boys who had been expelled from prep school; I served on committees; I headed campaigns. God was my refuge and He gave me a dear Christian friend in the Episcopal Church in Palm Beach. She encouraged me in my desire for God's way and we had daily Bible study for several years. Later, without consulting each other, we both resigned from the church and sought fellowship elsewhere. But that's getting ahead of my story.

With marriage number three out of the way, I opened a decorating business which was immediately successful. I had ideas and contacts. Furthermore, I liked working with people, and this gave me opportunities with both clients and employees. As I became more active in the church, I spoke more openly about religion, too.

One day, after overhearing me speak to an employee about Christ, an electrician whom I employed, followed me up the elevator to my office. He initiated a conversation about Jesus Christ and invited me to hear Ernest Tatham at a small Bible Chapel in West Palm Beach. I agreed to go, and it was a delightful experience. The special quality of this kind of Bible study captured my interest, and I returned again. These people knew Jesus Christ as I wanted to know Him. After I admitted this, God began to zero in on me with new truth about Himself.

Some time later I went to Austria and through a friend I met Mr. and Mrs. Fredrick Wood (who began the National Young Life Campaign in England about fifty years ago). We had many talks together about God and Jesus Christ, and I found this a welcome stimulus to my spiritual life. They introduced me to several of G. Campbell Morgan's books which initiated a genuine hunger in me to know more Truth. God was faithfully making Himself more real to me. When Joe Blinco held a Crusade in North Palm Beach in 1964 and gave a call for commitment, I went forward. I had no idea there was so much to know about God and His plan of redemption through Jesus Christ.

Meanwhile God was bringing pressures to bear on other areas of my life. Just as I began to get really excited about knowing Him after my visit to Austria, I found I had a malignant thyroid. God had to show me how "He works everything together for good for those who love Him. . . ." After He took care of that problem, He led me to close out my decorating business, assuring me that He had some other plan for me. There were so many loose ends. My life was still mixed up morally because I had accepted my peers' standard, and all my sins were respectable ones as far as I knew.

Some time later during a holiday in Europe I seized the opportunity to spend three weeks alone at a friend's home to read. My hunger to know God better had been often frustrated by a busy life. Here were three weeks alone just to read the Bible. Little did I know of what God was going to do in those weeks.

I began to read in Matthew and eventually came to chapter five where I read the words of Jesus, "But I say unto you, That whosoever looketh on a woman to lust after her hath committed adultery with her already in his heart." As lightning illuminates darkness, I saw myself in the eyes of God. God's standard was holiness, the purity and righteousness of Jesus Christ. My life passed before me in a flash of memory, and I saw myself as God must see me. I read on, "And if thy right eye offend thee, pluck it out . . ."

I wept for twenty-four hours over my sin. Then I felt forgiven. But action was demanded. The Bible said, ". . . pluck it out." I broke off an involved relationship, explaining the reality of Jesus Christ in my life and my experience of sins forgiven. Then for the first time His power came to my life and I had one goal — to live for Him.

Joyful Christian life began at fifty for me. He cleaned up my life morally and materially, and I became a student of the Word of God. The first fruits of this new-found relationship was the weekly Bible class in my home (taught by Ernest Tatham) for about twenty-two of my friends in Palm Beach. When God takes the blinders off your eyes, you see for the first time. And you see that everyone you know needs Him. Childhood friends have come back into my life in a remarkable way, and I've got such Good News to share with them.

I prayed that my two children might meet Christ, too. I took my daughter along with me to Capri that first summer. I also took along the tape recordings of our Bible studies, hoping I could start a group on Capri and use Mr. Tatham's teaching there. I never played a single recording, but during the summer my daughter became a member of God's family through faith in Jesus Christ. She has since led her five-year-old son to know Him. That God should allow me this joy is proof of His great mercy and grace.

When I first heard about Child Evangelism, I got excited about the possibilities latent in teaching children what the Bible said and introducing them to Jesus Christ. I knew that if I had known more of the Scriptures earlier in my life, a lot of personal heartache could have been avoided. We have begun two classes for children in our area now, and I've had the happy experience of teaching one of these. I have an outreach to adults through the Bible study, and now I can help these children, as well.

When I visited the Child Evangelism representative on the west coast of Florida and saw that he had a book store in his small living room, that gave me an idea. Why not begin one in my home in Palm Beach? My decorator's eye quickly remodeled my dining room into a French Library, stocked with Bibles and books. I'd have bookcases built around the walls, with good lighting over them, paint them a clear soft yellow with an antiqued finish. I'd leave the table in the middle so it could serve as a library or study table for all ages to use.

This vision has become a reality, and now on the door of my home in Palm Beach a small sign reads:

Good News Bible and Book Store
Hours: 10 until 7
Please walk in.

The sign is done in the colors of the wordless book — black, red, white and gold — for two reasons. First, these colors tell the story of salvation. Secondly, the profits from the store help support the work of Child Evangelism on our side of the state of Florida. I'm there Monday through Saturday, eager to talk about the books, to urge the browsers to read the Bible, and sometimes to share a cup of tea while I have the pleasure of telling what Jesus Christ has done for my life.

So much of my life story could have been different if I had known what the Bible says. I didn't know what His way was. I thought any way was His way without discernment. I thought I'd do anything for God — even be a slave of men. The devil uses sins which are "respectable" in our society to confuse us about His plan for us. That's why the Scriptures are so important in our lives.

But there's more to the story. My son, a college senior, flew to Florida for a two-day visit about a month after his sister became a Christian. "I want to see if all I've heard about her is true," he said. So we went over together to visit her. Later on the way to the airport, he said, "Well, seeing *is* believing. She *is* different."

"That's what the Gospel does for a person," I began. He knowingly assured me that he had taken a course in the synoptic gospels in school and knew all about it.

"Not gospels," I interjected, "The Gospel of the Lord Jesus Christ is what I'm talking about." And then with the simple wordless book I use in the children's classes, I told him the Good News of what Jesus had come to do for people like us — about hearts, black with sin, being washed clean by the blood of Jesus who died that we might have eternal life.

When I finished he was thoughtful and said he'd never

heard that before and he would have to think it over. Just before the plane took off I urged him not to delay a decision to ask Christ to take over his life. I waved good-by and he left.

For two months I didn't hear from him — and I learned a lot about prayer. Then at Thanksgiving time came the most beautiful letter I'd ever received from him. He poured out pages and pages of conviction of sin and need of God. I called him long distance at his fraternity house and spoke of the letter. "You're ready to become a Christian, Tim," I said.

He answered, "I already have, Mother."

I've never had a Thanksgiving like that one. Who but God can reach down into mixed up lives and bring order and peace!

Sometimes people ask, "At what point did you become a Christian?" God knows for certain; I don't. I only know I wanted Him since I was fourteen. He waited patiently for me as I bumbled through the years. I'll always be grateful for the people God brought into my life at all the right times. I've thanked Him often for my mother's maid and for the electrician who first invited me to the Bible-teaching church where I am now a member. And there have been so many friends since then to encourage my growth in the Lord. God's family is a very special thing. Now I want God to use me in the lives of the members of my community. Many of them are such innocent victims of plenty. Wealth often keeps people from facing life's ultimate issues by offering escape to new situations. You can go to a new place, buy a new toy or find a new marriage. But eventually escape is impossible, and sooner or later they realize what hollow people they are. That's when I want to be on hand to tell them about Jesus.

I'm awed as I look back over the confusion of my past life and see the mercy of God. The Samaritan woman (of John's gospel, chapter four) and I have so much in common. She was seeking in men what she could only find in Jesus. In a sense, I was seeking Him in all my husbands. I was looking for Someone who would love me as I was and make me what I should be. I found this in Jesus Christ. There is no real affection apart for Him. He not only accepts us and loves us, but He forgives us as well. "You are complete in him," said the Apostle Paul, and I know what he means.

16

Dorothy Galde

When I think of Dorothy Galde's life, I think of high winds, rough waters, but in the boat — peace. That neatly sums up her circumstances and her inner resources.

IN THE ANCIENT BOOK OF JOB Satan appeared before God and accused Job. He said, in effect, "No wonder Job trusts you. Look at all he has to make his life easy and comfortable. He doesn't know what trouble is!" You know the rest of the story — Job's loss, his physical misery, the contempt of those closest to him, and yet his steadfast words, "Though he slay me, yet will I trust him."

Job is an enigma to modern man. Philosophers still discuss what Job teaches about the origin of evil, about the problem of pain. Sometimes they miss the more profound conclusion: here is a man who knows God and trusts His character even when he can't understand what is happening.

Today some wear Satan's mask and sneer, "They don't know what life is about. No wonder they are content to believe in God. They sit there, unrelated to the world, with their easy answers. . . ." And then one meets a Dorothy Galde and journeys with her through a series of her *unanswerables,* and finds contemporary insights into Job, but more important meets a *God Who is Enough.*[1]

Attractive Dorothy Horton was a sophomore at Wheaton College when she first met Luke Penheiter and fell in love. Two dozen long-stemmed roses arrived at Christmas time to say, "I love you," confirming that feelings were mutual. College Tower bells rang to announce their engagement, and two shiny-faced people looked at life and said, "World, here we come!"

Luke was a senior pre-med student, so when Spring came he said his farewells to the joys of a small college and headed for medical school at the University of North Dakota. The depression was in full swing, and Luke had to work as well as study. But love is invincible, and miles away Dorothy stuck to her school work at Wheaton until graduation — a long two years.

Still they couldn't marry. No money. But Luke did transfer to Northwestern Medical School for his junior year, and Dorothy planned to teach in the Chicago area. At least they would be together and the letter-writing part of their romance would be over. When the Board of Education told Dorothy they had no teaching posts open, the new college graduate found herself a job as a waitress at the Lawson YMCA. She earned the whole sum of $7.35 every two weeks, plus two meals a day. Her room cost three dollars a week, and at the end of two weeks she had the grand sum of $1.35 to squander on riotous living. "It's great what education can do for you," Dorothy wrote home.

Within a few months she found a better job as a waitress in the Women's University Club. Her salary was an unheard of kind of affluence — fifty dollars a month and three meals a day! Her father wrote back about this news: "Dot, we're

---

[1]A translation of one of the Old Testament names for God, *El Shaddai.*

thankful to God for your new job. If you walk with Him you will find He always supplies what you need, even though it may not be exactly as you planned."

The new salary made possible new wedding finery. Dorothy bought a second-hand sewing machine and spent her spare moments putting together the trousseau of her dreams. Guests at the club soon discovered the cause of her radiance and wedding gifts began to arrive. Dorothy and her sister Lillian were planning a double wedding; excitement ran high. It was the glowing, young love experience every girl hopes life will hold for her.

They were married that summer and the following year was all the special things a first year of marriage should be. Then Luke graduated from medical school and went off to intern at St. Luke's Hospital in Duluth, Minnesota. They still had no money, and it was imperative that Dorothy continue working. Except for holiday times, eight hundred miles and little money kept them separated until the year of internship was over.

Luke had planned from boyhood to join his uncle's practice in a little town in Minnesota. So the Penheiters rented a ramshackle old house, remodeling and furnishing it as they could afford to, and settled down to the life of a small town practice. Dorothy unpacked the wedding gifts and learned how to cook on the wood stove that stood in the kitchen. She also learned what it meant to be a doctor's wife.

One night when Luke was called out to deliver a baby, Dorothy was seized with terrible pains. She didn't call Luke because, after all, he was delivering a baby. She took anacin instead and wrestled with the situation until the clock showed 8 a.m. Then she called the hospital. Luke's uncle shortly thereafter performed an appendectomy on Dorothy, and found the appendix about to burst. Dorothy almost didn't make it through that ordeal, and young Dr. Penheiter had a new awareness of God's help in the practice of medicine.

Three months passed. The Penheiters had the world by the tail. It was a satisfying, contented life. Then one morning Dorothy woke Luke up a little late, and hurried downstairs to get the big black stove functioning. Luke appeared just as breakfast was ready. He looked peculiar somehow, but in the morning flurry to get breakfast on the table, Dorothy didn't ask questions. She turned from the stove to find him crumpled to the floor. He whispered for her to call Uncle LeRoy. She rang and rang. The telephone was out of order. With great effort Luke wrote and sealed a note to the doctor and Dorothy tore out of the house with it, praying all the way, her feet literally flying down the dirt road to the hospital, terror filling her heart. Something was happening to her life, to her love.

The note said, "Suspect cerebral hemorrhage." Young Dr. Penheiter died that day.

Something inside Dorothy died, too. But it wasn't her faith in God. If she ever knew He was real and not a figment of her imagination it was now. He seemed to come to her with a strong undergirding — "underneath are the everlasting arms." Job's words came from her mouth as if from a far place, "The Lord gave, and the Lord has taken away; blessed be the name of the Lord." The hurt of it was awful, but she knew it was true.

Stormy days followed when Dorothy asked *why*? and found no answers. She had to face self-pity head on and do something about it. Her parents had taught her the words of Scripture as a child, she had studied at Wheaton, she had personally trusted Christ, and now this heritage came to her rescue. Never had God's words been so sweet, so reviving, and never had she needed His fellowship more.

Dorothy says, "I was now learning more per square inch of life than I had ever discovered in all the rest of my years put together. I set up a new partnership with God. I was a pretty immature partner, but He was always there, ready for consultation."

Dorothy decided she had done enough living to write the Great American Novel, and decided to return to Wheaton to do it. Instead she worked in the college dining hall and, maybe subconsciously as time went on, hoped that this setting might provide her with someone else to fill the longing she felt within herself. She took some additional course work in food planning and got experience supervising food production. God was leading her in another direction, and had some talks with her about His sufficiency if she never married again.

When she was offered the position of Restaurant Manager of the YMCA Hotel in Chicago, Dorothy threw herself into her career. Remarriage was no longer a live option. This was it, and a new adventure began — an absorbing one. She worked long hours, enrolled in courses in management, and often fell into bed too exhausted to be lonely.

Eventually a personable young man named Lloyd Galde noticed the young Mrs. Penheiter. Lloyd Galde was attending George Williams College, expecting to go into YMCA work after graduation. He was working his way through school with a night cashier's job at the Y Hotel. One night when Dorothy had been working late, Lloyd came out of his cashier's cage and tried to whip up a bowling game with some of the clerks. Unsuccessful, he finally turned to Dorothy and asked with a grin, "Would you care to bowl for an hour and get that restaurant look off your face?"

If she looked that bad, Dorothy decided she could use some bowling. After the first line, an impudent Lloyd Galde asked, "Mrs. Penheiter, would you like me to teach you *how* to bowl?" She did and he did, and it was a refreshing change from the grind of work in which she had been so absorbed.

It was also a safe relationship. A girl back home had jilted Lloyd, and he was interested in staying "free." Dorothy had closed her mind to thoughts of remarrying and was going places in her career. Occasionally Lloyd would ask her out, and they had an easy, relaxed companionship. Neither tried to impress the other. They became such casually good friends that he got the habit of calling her every night at ten o'clock just to chat over the day's events. And sometimes they sent each other silly notes.

They talked about Jesus Christ, too. Lloyd was interested and realized something was lacking in his life. He recognized the great gulf between them in matters of faith, and began to investigate knowing Jesus Christ on his own. Dorothy never pushed him, and his entrance into the family of God by personally trusting Jesus Christ was his own decision.

The staggering truth of what was happening hit Dorothy with a wallop when Lloyd took off for a vacation. She missed his 10 p.m. phone calls and his notes. Then a postcard came from Washington:

> Either the Washington Monument isn't all it's cracked up to be or nothing looks good to me unless you're looking at it with me.

They were in love. She hadn't planned it that way. She was older than he was by three years and he was the same height as she. "I'll never be able to wear high heels again," Dorothy moaned.

Lloyd countered with, "Yes, and you're the assistant manager of the hotel, and I'm just a cashier. You're making more money than I am, and I haven't even finished college."

Their hearts spoke louder than their arguments, and in the months ahead they planned to marry. Shortly after Lloyd had become the assistant manager of a hotel in Kenosha, he got official greetings from the President of the United States, calling him into service. Wedding plans ground to a halt. Dorothy had had all her dreams swept away once before, and she was not eager to repeat the pattern of separation she had known. The Air Force, Lloyd's first choice, was not taking married men. They tried to find out through prayer what God had in mind for them to do.

The Pearl Harbor incident changed the Air Force ruling. They were taking men, all men, married men. Dorothy and Lloyd changed their ruling, too, and were married on New Year's Day.

Twenty-seven days later Lloyd went into service. Within the first year Dorothy resigned her job in Chicago and went home to live with her parents. Morning nausea and restaurant kitchen smells did not mix. Lloyd came home on furlough at the end of October to welcome Peter, their first-born son.

Peter and his mother joined Lloyd at bases in California and Texas, where he completed his glider training. Eventually morning nausea sent Dorothy and Peter home to her parents again, where she delivered son number two, Daniel. Lloyd wrote her a note from the airbase and said, "After your Dad called I took up the plane and had myself a couple of barrel rolls and a few loops to celebrate the occasion. There wasn't enough room for my new chest expansion on the ground."

Lloyd received his orders for overseas duty shortly after he settled his family in a small house in a country town not too far from her parents. Her sister Lillian and family lived only a few houses away. The arrangement was the best possible, and Lloyd went off to war in the springtime.

In the summer of 1944 polio scared the whole community. Dorothy took extra precautions with the children, keeping them out of the heat and staying away from crowds. Hospitals were full, and she was afraid — and tired. At first she thought her own problem was simply nervous fatigue. The two children were a handful and she did miss Lloyd. Word from England was scarce with the invasion of Europe underway. The morning Dorothy couldn't move either leg more than an inch off the bed, both she and the doctor knew that her problem was polio.

The telegram they sent to Lloyd arrived while he was out on a dangerous mission landing a glider of troops in Holland for the Arnheim invasion. That he returned to England at all to receive the message was a miracle of sorts. Contrary to Dorothy's wishes, the telegram mentioned only a light case of polio, and the Air Force was reluctant to release Lloyd until they had more information. Between battle fatigue and concern for his family, Lloyd suffered through some discouraging days. Eventually he got in touch with the right people and was sent home.

Dorothy's polio was no light case. She was quarantined because they feared contagion. She was lonely, and the pain was unbearable. Paralyzed from the waist down, even her back and neck were affected. Her arms were limp as spaghetti, and her internal organs refused to function normally. Every four hours nurses changed her Kenny packs, and the moist burning sensation brought the only relief she knew, and that was gone within minutes.

Her world was rocking badly. No word from Lloyd. How were the children? The awful pain spasms continued for almost two weeks, but it helped when Dorothy heard that the pain was a hopeful sign that the nerves and muscles were fighting back.

Dorothy did not hear the doctors tell her father that she would never walk again. Dorothy said, "I have always been thankful that I did not know what was up ahead. The Lord taught me that when Luke died. Each day I found Him sufficient, and so I took life just one day at a time."

The days ahead brought a joyful reunion with Lloyd, and hours of such awful torture that the patients called the physiotherapy rooms "Buchenwald." The pain involved in the rehabilitation of her muscles caught Dorothy off guard. She had thought the painful part was over, but it seemed only the beginning. First the therapist lifted her leg only an inch from the bed, then an inch and a half, then two inches, forcing the muscles to work. The pain was agonizing, but in another sense, it was almost a pleasure because it meant something was alive in those seemingly lifeless limbs. The doctor said, "Stay in there and pitch, gal. Concentrate as you've never concentrated before."

Dorothy started *thinking* movement to consciously try to reestablish what was once involuntary motion. It was a struggle of mind over matter. She hung onto God in desperation for daily strength.

Dorothy told her Dad one day, "My pain and loneliness have brought me closer to the Lord than I have ever been in my life. Oh, Daddy I couldn't do anything without Him. The effort the slightest move takes is too much for me; I have to hang onto Him."

Her wise father said, "Faith and prayer, Dorothy. These are the two hands God holds out to us to give us courage when our spirit sags."

What a miracle it was the day the nurse slid Dorothy off the bed to stand on her own two feet. By pushing the knee out in the back she was able to keep from toppling. Every muscle movement, every bit of balance, was no longer involuntary, but required intense concentration. If she leaned the slightest bit off center, she fell to the floor. Fifty pounds lighter, she felt like a bag of bones, and her body took on a new color — black and blue. The hard marble floor of the hospital became her enemy.

Even the tiniest hint of victory was sweet. She kept constantly before her the hope of a reunited family. Lloyd would soon be discharged and the babies could be brought back home. Hydrotherapy marked a real milestone and she began to see some progress each day. The right leg suffered more than the left. The quadreceps of her right leg, the large muscle that goes from the thigh to the knee, never came back. When Lloyd was discharged, she found his shoulder the perfect hanging-on-to height when she tried to walk. They laughed about the day she had moaned over his being the same height as she.

Dorothy went home to her parents for Christmas. Her whole family (except for Peter and Danny) gathered at her Mother and Dad's — twenty of them. After all the gifts had been opened, Dorothy announced her gift. "There is one more present," she said, as all eyes turned on her. Placing her hands firmly on the arms of her chair, she pushed herself to her feet. She dared not look at anyone for fear of breaking her concentration. With great effort she walked across the few steps to Lloyd, who caught her in his arms.

It was the best part of Christmas for all of them — so wonderful, they wept. Dorothy recalls, "No one knew quite what to say at this victory. The hush of the room was punctuated only by the blowing of noses."

Lloyd spent long hours at the hospital, learning how to give massages and muscle exercises. Domestic help was hard to find because everyone was working in the local war plants, but after weeks of prayer and searching, Lloyd was able to take his wife home. He flew to Milwaukee to get Peter, now two and a half. It had been six months since Dorothy had seen him. Danny, with relatives in Duluth, was her only lack.

Dorothy's progress was slow. A few months after she was home, the orthopedic clinic recommended a brace to strengthen her right leg. It was a dreadful thing and threw her off balance by upsetting the system with which she had learned to walk. When she fell with the brace, she sounded like the "Anvil Chorus." She had to learn to manage all over again and conquer her fear of falling, especially since she was expecting a third child.

One night late in May, Lloyd and Dorothy were awakened at 1:30 A.M. to discover a fire in their house. Dorothy had never walked in her bare feet, but she did that night. Lloyd ran downstairs to investigate, while Dorothy worked her way into Peter's room. Pounding back up the stairs, Lloyd grabbed Peter out of his crib, covering him with a blanket, and ran down the stairs, calling an immediate return for Dorothy. He knew he had to work fast.

Dorothy sensed from Lloyd's actions that the danger was serious — that there was no time to lose. She flung herself to the floor and crawled over to a little door at the head of the stairs. As she peered out, the fire swept up, burning her face and singing her hair. She pulled back and decided the feet-first approach would be most practical. Wrestling her weak leg into position, she pushed hard with her arms, and slid down the stairs. The stairway was like a flue, and the fire roared above her.

She was dragging herself across the hot floor to the door as Lloyd came, black with soot and smoke, to rescue her. An hour later firetrucks were still sending water high into the flames as the ambulance drove both Lloyd and Dorothy off to the hospital. They lost all their possessions, but the family was safe. Dorothy was hospitalized for two weeks. Her three-month pregnancy was unharmed, and although her face was swollen and bandaged for days, no sign of a scar remained after the healing.

The months following the fire were full of promise and

excitement. Lloyd began selling insurance, Danny came home, Teddy was born by Caesarean section, and the Galdes built a new house. Keeping up with three children wasn't easy, but the house had been planned to make it as simple as possible.

Dorothy fell on her knee during this time and it swelled badly. The doctor was not optimistic. He frankly told Dorothy that he doubted that she would ever walk again. The swelling persisted and the leg throbbed. Then she fell again and the fluid broke. The knee went down to normal size. The doctor had no explanation. God who had rescued her out of the paws of polio had done it again.

Lloyd and Dorothy had always wanted a girl, but the doctor had told them after Teddy's birth that Dorothy's child-bearing days were over. A friend, alone except for her eighteen-month-old daughter, was dying of a malignancy. She asked Lloyd and Dorothy if they would consider adopting her daughter. They talked to the Lord a long time about it, facing up to the grave responsibility of this move. Negative reasons were numerous, but still the Galdes felt compelled to take her. Brown-haired, brown-eyed Susie joined the family of boys.

Dorothy's cup of blessing was running over — a reunited family, a new home, a new car, and now a new baby girl. These were good years. God had restored what had seemed to be lost and gave a new beginning.

Only one thing plagued Dorothy's existence. She had learned to live with her polio handicap and her walking was improving, even though it was a slow process. Her problem was a constant sinus condition that dogged her every breath. Winters, fall and spring in the north were misery.

One night when they were doing dishes together, Lloyd said, "Honey, I just can't see you caged up here winter after winter. Ice and snow are so dangerous for you. And besides that, it just doesn't seem sensible for you to spend what energy you have struggling with a sinus condition. What would you think about moving to a hot, dry climate?"

It was a tremendous undertaking, and if they had known

all the future held they might never have ventured out. Leaving family behind was the worst part. Lloyd was promised a good opening in Dallas, Texas in the insurance business and they left the day after Christmas. The children called the move, "The Exodus to Texadus."

They found a beautiful home (with an acre of land and two creeks) and moved in, but despite hours of hard work and faithfulness, the insurance business failed. In seven months they had to sell their home and rent a smaller place. Everything about that experience hurt. They knew God hadn't moved them to Texas to spank them, and so once again, they were driven by love to trust His character when they could not understand.

The years that followed were full of changes, crises and love. And it was love that made the difference — their love for God and each other, and the sure confidence of His love for them. The Galdes call them happy years, but they were not uneventful ones. The diary of events reads so easily. How much heartache or joy is hidden in simple sentences!

— A business manager's job at a Christian camp opens up for Lloyd. Crude facilities, but exciting ministry to young people.
— Lloyd moves family to camp site. Live in trailer until house is built for them by friends.
— Lloyd resigns from camp staff after three years. His vision is larger than his opportunity.
— Homeless, jobless, moneyless.
— The Galdes meet a couple interested in developing new Christian camp, begin to pray with them about it.
— Dorothy has severe asthma attacks; rescued by oxygen and intravenous injections.
— Move into double garage of friend.
— Lloyd takes job as salesman.
— Dorothy hospitalized with bronchial asthma. Cortisone tried; effective.

— House loaned to them, rent free.
— Three couples meet to pray for new camp, called Sky Ranch, Inc.
— Camp board forms, five interested members.
— Find camp property, begin day camp program first summer.
— Dorothy begins teaching job in Duncanville.
— Move to sixteenth home in Duncanville. Lloyd drives to Dallas daily.
— Peter, during football check-up, discovered to have spondylolisthesis, necessitating spinal fusion. Operation costs, twelve hundred dollars.
— Lloyd enrolls in college to finish two years.
— More camp development. Fantastic answers to prayer.
— Lloyd graduates from college.
— Lloyd becomes elementary principal in Duncanville.
— Lloyd develops severe pollen allergy. Doctor insists he resign and move to Sky Ranch.
— Family moves near Sky Ranch.

The Galdes got used to trusting God for big things in crises. They believed He could do anything, and God used them to spark the faith of others in the Sky Ranch project. Lloyd and Dorothy could have said, "We've got enough concerns of our own. We can't get involved in the pioneering chore of beginning a camp, of praying in wells, buildings and campers." But the Galdes aren't that kind of people. They've proved God so many times, that proving Him once more seemed part of the Plan, and Sky Ranch got off the ground successfully.

Ten years have passed since then. Sky Ranch is still their prayer concern, but they are no longer actively involved in its operation. The children are grown now. Susan is married with a baby of her own. Peter hopes to teach history someday on a collegiate level. Dan is married and presently serving with a pararescue team in the air force. Ted attends Arizona

State College, majoring in speech. Lloyd and Dorothy both teach school in Prescott, Arizona, and they are just completing the building of house number four; it will be their twenty-third home. Dorothy also sings in the choir, teaches Sunday school, is enrolled in graduate work and continues to love the stream of people who come into her life.

A friend recently said, "Dottie's mind goes at ninety miles an hour and her feet at ten." Dorothy walks today by the grace of God. If one knee bends and the other isn't properly set, she still falls to the floor with a thud. The cortisone she has taken daily for ten years to control asthma causes bones to become more brittle and falls to become more fearful. "But," says Dorothy, "in ten years of teaching I have fallen badly on the school grounds but once. Isn't the Lord gracious?'

I asked her how she interprets all that has happened in her life. She quoted Charles Kettering's words, "Never bring me anything but bad news; good news weakens me." Then she went on to explain the supreme lesson of her life. *In everything give thanks for this is the will of God in Christ Jesus concerning you.* I Thessalonians 5:18

Dorothy says, "In some strange way I have had to learn this lesson repeatedly. The more the Lord has given me, the less tender my heart is in thankfulness to Him. This seems to be human nature. It came home to me with appalling clarity as I taught an Old Testament survey this year, how many men worshiped God in their youth, but departed from Him in their old age, often because of the abundance of His goodness to them.

"I am exceedingly, abundantly glad to be here, to be alive and warm and breathing each day, not because I think this is all there is to life, but because I know this means there is something for me to *do* for Him."

All things work together for good (Romans 8:28) is a very quotable verse, easier to say than to experience. When Dorothy says it is in every thread of the cloth of life she is weaving, she does not speak glibly.

There is something beautiful about thankfulness, courage and vitality. These words describe Dorothy Galde, but only because she knows God and trusts Him. There is a world of difference between knowing *about* Someone and knowing Him personally. Job's words come to mind,

> I know that thou canst do all things,
> and that no purpose of thine can be thwarted. . . .
> I had heard of thee by the hearing of the ear,
> but now my eye sees thee. . . .[2]

---

[2]Job 42:2, 5, RSV.

17

Jean Gross Coombs

Jean Gross Coombs and her history professor husband, Dr. Norman Coombs, live near the campus of Rochester Institute of Technology in New York state. Jean's story is one of the sovereignty of God, for He called her to Himself when she was a child and kept her trusting Him even when she was discouraged from doing so. Jean has a natural spontaneity which enables her to enjoy life's good things — plus an unusual gift for sharing them with her husband.

I CANNOT REMEMBER a time in my life when I wasn't reaching out for God. As far back as I can think into the fuzzy, distant realms of memory, I see myself lying in bed at night thinking and wondering about God. I wondered if He existed. I wondered if He knew about me. I wondered if He loved me. I wondered how to get to know Him. As I think back now to those earliest moments and the times of questioning and conflict and joy that followed through the years, I realize why some unknown poet wrote,

Jean Gross Coombs

I sought the Lord, and afterward I knew
He moved my soul to seek Him, seeking me;
It was not I that found, O Savior true;
No, I was found of Thee.

When I was about two and a half years old, my mother died and then Father strangely disappeared. Nobody explained because they said I was too young to understand. But suddenly Grandmother was my new mother and my uncle was my new father. It didn't seem too strange, but it was probably more upsetting than I remember. Grandfather lived with us too, but I didn't get to know him very well. He spent a lot of time in his room, and later I learned about his love for the bottle and his long lost weekends. Uncle John was my favorite and I called him Daddy. He was young and fun and a real playmate, whereas Grandma was nervous and didn't like too much noise.

I don't know where I heard about God in order to wonder about Him, but in addition to trying to figure it all out by myself, I asked my new family. Grandma said He existed and Daddy said He didn't. I was always on Daddy's side because he was my friend, but this puzzled me. Somehow it seemed that God must exist, but Daddy was so smart and so confident, and Grandma was nervous and so unsure. I was apparently old enough to begin Sunday school, and it was decided that I should go. Grandma thought all children should go to Sunday school, but Daddy thought this was the worst possible thing for a child. Somehow Grandma won the battle. Thank God she did.

At Sunday school a whole new wonderful world opened up. I learned about Jesus and about the little children gathered around Him, even when other grownups tried to get rid of them. And about little Samuel who said, "Speak, Lord, for thy servant hears." And about baby Moses in the bulrushes and how God saved him and kept him to lead the chosen people. I learned to sing songs about Jesus loving all the children in the world. I learned to recite verses from the Bible, like "Even a child is known by his doings. . . ."

And the teachers were sure that children were very precious to God and that God loved each of us. I was glad about that.

Grandma always said the teachers were right, but she made me angry so often I didn't care what she thought. Daddy said the teachers were wrong, and I idolized him, and continued to lie in bed at night and wonder. And I must have prayed. I'm sure I asked the Lord to show me whom to believe, but I think I was beginning to know.

Daddy and I often took long walks together and had long talks. Somehow the subject came around again and again to the existence of God. I would ask, "Daddy, don't you *really* believe there is a God?"

He would say, "Of course not," in his honest, straightforward way.

"But Daddy," I challenged, looking around us as we walked, "if there isn't a God where did all the trees come from?"

"From seeds."

"But . . . (and somehow I could think this one through even at a tender age) then where did the seeds come from?"

"From trees."

What could a small child answer to an explanation like this? It seemed so final. "But Daddy," I asked, feeling like I was about to be the winner in this argument, "where did the *first* tree come from?"

"From the first seed."

And now the final triumph, "But where did the first *seed* come from?"

"From the first tree." He was so sure. And he was my beloved daddy.

By the grace of God and the faithfulness of Sunday school and Daily Vacation Bible School teachers I came to know more and more about my Heavenly Father, and how He had sent Jesus to die for everyone, including me. We were taught to pray aloud together and memorize many, many verses from the Bible, to sing hymns and choruses, to tell others about Jesus Christ and to know Him personally as Saviour and Lord. And lying in bed at night became more a time of genuine communion with the God I was learning to love and less a time of questioning turmoil. Somehow nothing Daddy said could take this away. I loved Daddy very much, but I loved God more.

Toward the end of high school a new element of Christianity came into my life. I met several fellow students who spent their weekends going to Christian meetings, instead of to dances and movies. This seemed a bit fanatical, but I was attracted by their sincerity even though I didn't intend for some of their strange ideas to rub off. I began to attend some of their meetings, area Christian Endeavor rallies and day camps.

At such a day camp, held on one Saturday early in May, a very strange but meaningful thing happened. After a day of hiking and fun, we had a meeting filled with vigorous music and personal stories of how people had come to know Christ. Then came time for the speaker. I had never heard anything quite like his sermon. He told a story about a little girl whose father asked her to throw a toy pearl necklace into the fire. She loved her toy and resisted, but eventually she obeyed her father and threw the necklace away. Her father rewarded her obedience with a genuine pearl necklace. We were asked to do the same with regard to Jesus Christ. We were asked to throw away our worldly life and take His life and live only for Him. The minister asked everybody who had never done this before to raise his hand and give himself completely to Christ.

My heart began to pound and even though I had known the Lord for years and had grown to trust and love Him, I felt that since I had never raised my hand, I must. I wanted more than anything in the world to live completely for Jesus Christ, so I raised my hand and said I wanted to throw away the useless pearls and receive the really valuable ones. Thinking back now, I honestly don't know what to think about that meeting or about that illustration, but I remember that something happened to me — at least psychologically — that evening.

That, however, was the first of many such evangelistic

services which served, unfortunately, to raise a new area of confusion and doubt. For several years I was besieged with questions about my salvation since personal salvation was always the message preached by the speaker. All would be going along beautifully. I was sure I loved God and belonged to Him. I would tell others about Him. Then I would go to one of these services and end the evening in terrible turmoil. "Are you *sure* that you have accepted Jesus Christ as your Saviour?" "Do you *know* that if you get killed by a car on the way home tonight you will go to heaven to be with God forever?" Since I had raised my hand and had prayed to the Lord many times to save me, I always felt it unnecessary to "go forward" but the trip home was usually one of torment. I feared every car lest it plunge me into a "Christless eternity." I could hardly get home fast enough to fall on my knees by my bedside and re-accept Christ.

To add to the torment of these years was the problem that if I shared this with the family it would only confirm their suspicions about Christianity. And if I told other Christians I would get Bible verses and loving exhortations about making sure again. One of the verses that always made everything worse was the one about the Spirit bearing witness with our spirit that we *are* the children of God. Didn't anyone understand the uncertainties of a teenager's heart? But one Christian finally did show me a verse that really helped. It was Philippians 1:6, "Being certain that He which has begun a good work in you will perform it until the day of Jesus Christ." And the era of doubt was beginning to end.

It ended permanently (except for a couple of later incidents) when I discovered the ministry of Donald Grey Barnhouse at Tenth Presbyterian Church in Philadelphia. Here was a man of God who taught substance, who expounded the Scriptures in great detail, with intelligence and humor. I began to go to church every Sunday night and sit through long sermons, digging into Bible passages and learning about the character of God as I had never seen it before. I was learning so much I didn't even want to talk with people after the service. I would go alone, take voluminous notes, and leave alone for my hour-long trip home. I left those meetings filled with joy that such a God existed, that such a world existed, that I existed. I no longer eyed every car suspiciously lest it whisk me off to Hell, but I eyed the world around me with increasing confidence. I was only a teenager, but I recognized this ministry of upbuilding. It was a turning point in my life.

Time for college came. Despite the new peace God had given me, the same old problem, not quite dead, reared its head again. I was afraid. Could I keep my faith or was Daddy really right after all? At this point I couldn't bear the thought of losing this relationship with Christ. I chose a Christian college just to be "safe." Since Daddy was sending me and had to approve the school, it was difficult to find one that suited his standards. Houghton seemed good enough because there were a sufficient number of Ph.D's on the faculty and because it was fully accredited.

I went to Houghton College, torn between my joy at knowing God and the fear of losing Him. I felt that Christian teachers and Christian students and an atmosphere free from temptations could keep me. But, oh dear! Houghton was in a rural area; I had always lived in a big city. Houghton was very strict; I had always had a great deal of freedom. Houghton was "holiness" in doctrinal position; I was just coming to a solid belief in a God who was holding onto me no matter what.

I learned that it is not the external that defiles a man, but that which comes from inside. I learned that many Christians are confused and haven't sorted out their fears, ignorance or sin. And I realized that being told to go to church and pray and sing Christian songs somehow made me want to run away from it all like I never had wanted to before. Strange that a Christian environment could turn one from God, but it was happening. I was becoming flippant about the sacred things of God and I grieved the Holy Spirit enough to know that I must leave this environment which apparently brought out the worst in me. Of the possibilities of colleges to which to transfer, Ohio State had the best financial arrangement. So I went to Ohio State, the opposite extreme from Houghton. Daddy was sure I would see the light now.

It was at Ohio State that I really began to find myself. Those two years were ones of exciting and expanding horizons. I found the campus to be the most challenging and interesting mission field imaginable. Instead of terrible sinners lurking in every corner to lure me into sin, I found lonely sinners asking about the meaning of life. I found confused sinners. I found delightful, loving sinners. I *liked* them. Many became close friends, not merely "projects" to "work on." And Christian fellowship became a meaningful unity with others who loved Jesus Christ and had perhaps only that in common.

Little wonder that graduation came much too soon, and I left college feeling that I had just begun to see and hear and feel what being a Christian was all about. I had caught a vision. I had not lost my faith but instead had found myself. And now I wanted to spend the rest of my life with college people telling them that God was real and they didn't have to throw Him out of their lives like Daddy did, but that the more they learned, the more they would see of Him.

Two years later, after a year at Biblical Seminary and a year of working at a Christian residence in New York, the vision was still there. The call to student work was even stronger, and God allowed me to go back into the campus mission field again, this time as a staff worker with Inter-Varsity Christian Fellowship. I was assigned to Wisconsin and northern Illinois, and for four and a half years I lived out of a suitcase and visited students in colleges. I saw God work in many lives, in many situations. He worked in me. I saw Him give me love for students who were terribly limited in their horizons and some who were boring as people. He reached through barriers and gave oneness. He gave vision to many. He gave eternal life. I saw miracle after miracle. Being a staff worker with Inter-Varsity was like being in the middle of a job that was always too big and too hard and too unpleasant, but finding every time that the Holy Spirit supplied power and joy and anything else that was needed.

But as I traveled around and stayed in many Christian homes, something else began to happen. I wanted a Christian home, too. I wanted more and more to find a man to love, to have my own home. I tried to squelch this longing, but it was getting stronger constantly. As the battle raged inside me, it became apparent that God was leading me into marriage or else the devil was waging an all-out war to ruin my effectiveness. I asked God repeatedly to renew my call to student work, to deliver me from distraction, but whenever an eligible man came into my life, the battle raged afresh. I still loved students and still thought of the campus as a mission field, but how I longed to share this call with a husband.

Then one day, after many disappointments, God hinted to me that my old friend Norm was the one. Norm was a student I had met my first year in Wisconsin when he was a college senior. Now he was working on his Ph.D. in history and planning to go into college teaching. We were the best of friends. We spent hours together having long talks over Italian salads and pizza. When I visited town he took me out to an occasional movie, a meal or a concert. He phoned often and we had good discussions on the telephone. But he wasn't anyone I was thinking about in terms of marriage because he was younger than I, shorter than I, and — totally blind. So for four years we had spent hours learning and growing together as Christians. We liked each other very much, but there was no attraction that could lead to marriage.

But one day the thought occurred to me — and it occurred very clearly as though it was God's idea — that this might be the one God had for me. I remember saying aloud, "Oh *no,* Lord, not Norm." But then I recalled that I had told the Lord a few days before (reaching about in my mind for what I considered the ultimate suffering) that I would go to the middle of Africa and live among snakes and bugs and teach little children in an orphanage if He wanted me to. But God would have to work in me to make me willing if this sort of thing was His will. So I transferred the request, changing the orphanage in Africa to marrying Norm. I said, "Lord, I will marry Norm if that is your will IF you will change my attitude towards him and his blindness and give me the kind of love for him I'd need to marry him."

And within one week I couldn't get Norm out of my mind. I thought of him constantly. I missed him when he wasn't around. I waited eagerly for him to telephone. And when, at the end of the summer, he asked me to pray about marrying him, I answered, "I have been — all summer." It took another month of agonizing to bring the willingness to pray about it to a positive commitment for life, but when the "yes" came, it came with joy and genuine confidence that this was God's doing.

Norm hasn't always been blind. When he was eight years old he and another boy were playing together, throwing sticks at each other. One of the sticks went into Norm's right eye and that eye lost all its sight. The doctors feared a possible sympathetic reaction in the other eye, and therefore removed the bad eye in the hope of saving the good one. However, over a period of a year, despite treatments and operations, the reaction took place. During that year his mother spent a great deal of time with him fixing visual images in his mind, such as geographical maps and colors. Norm's parents know God and by His grace and the prayers of others, they were able to accept this tragedy to their only child without bitterness.

Norm is a whole person to whom all of life is inter-related. I think this is part of what drew me to him. He enjoys people and experiences, and even visual things such as paintings which are described to him. He has an emotional stability that comes from his loving Christian home where he and his parents shared many wonderful times together as friends. He is very good for me. He gives me balance and helps me see things in the proper perspective.

Norm is obviously independent physically or he could not

handle himself in the business of living and being a professor. He is also independent emotionally in that he thinks for himself and doesn't let others influence him unless their ideas make sense as he thinks them through. His intelligence, sensitivity to life, humor, and moral integrity add to his spiritual stature and continue to impress me. I placed them side by side with the physical handicap of blindness. He was not the man of my dreams, but he was much more. Isn't that like a loving Father to do this for me?

We have been married for nearly seven years now and have a beautiful little daughter. God has given us love for each other and united love for many others. I have found Norm's blindness to be a very painful subject many times. I can't forget about it totally any more than he can. But we have grown and learned much together through difficult times and times of great joy. Norm has been a source of stability and constant intellectual challenge, helping me sensibly and Biblically when my deep-rooted proneness to doubt God has reappeared. And I have been his eyes.

God has kept His hand on me. He has always been there — from those earliest moments when I lay in bed at night and wondered. And I thank Him because He has really kept me.

> I find, I walk, I love;
> But O the whole of love is but my answer
> Lord to Thee!
> For Thou wert long beforehand with my soul;
> Always Thou lovedst me.

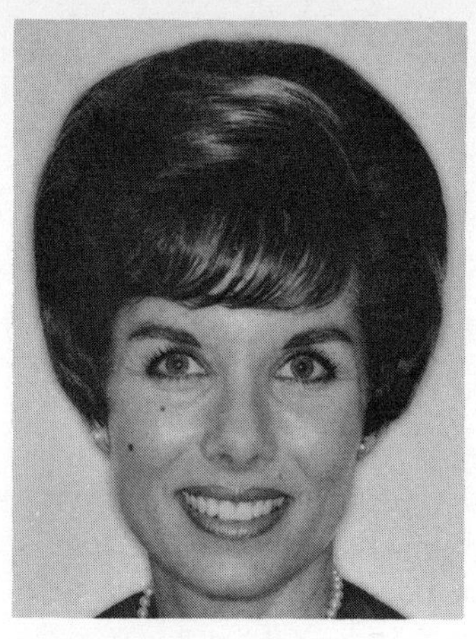

18

Colleen Evans

"Youth is not enough. And love is not enough. And success is not enough. And, if we could achieve it, enough would not be enough."[1] *Colleen Townsend, as a young starlet in Hollywood, felt the awful emptiness of this truth. When she met God in Jesus Christ, she found He was Enough.*

I DON'T HAVE a position. I'm in dynamic motion."

A neat character capsule describing Colleen Townsend Evans, this quotation is one of her favorites.[2] Colleen lives in the vital *now,* not in past memories. She is on the move, growing, learning and living. Some reporters and their readers are still standing in the theater wings looking for her, unwilling to let loose of her movie-actress image, an image they keep conjuring up. But Colleen is way out ahead of them. That was a distant, good yesterday. Today

---

[1]Mignon McLaughlin in *The Atlantic Monthly.*

[2]A quotation she first heard from Joe Blinco of the Billy Graham Team.

is far more exciting because she is "pressing on toward the goal."

But all the world wants a heroine from out of a story book, especially one as pretty as Colleen. People have a strange ability to make someone else's life seem more beautiful than their own. Yet when Colleen Evans tells her story she does so as matter-of-factly as you would tell yours. She is not interested in being a pin-up girl, but a flesh-and-blood woman who loves God and wants to please Him.

A mother and a grandfather were Colleen's family in her growing up years. A strict family with definite standards they were determined to bring Colleen up in a sensible, loving household. Her mother, an attractive, eligible woman, gave herself to being Colleen's mother. She married again only after Colleen was grown. It was a secure, unthreatened home as far as Colleen was concerned.

Her mother was a "down-to-earth" kind of person who did not cater to exaggerated ideas about one's own importance. Right from the beginning the stress was on what was inside a person, not on how one looked on the outside. The effects of this are evident today in the woman who is now Mrs. Louis Evans.

Although Colleen was a beautiful child, her mother never exploited this. The family had very little material wealth, and thus there was no temptation to overdress or pamper her daughter. Colleen says, "She wouldn't have done so, even if she could. She just wasn't that kind of a mother. Even when I was in the movies she was always the exact opposite of the typical pushy stage-mother type."

When a Mormon family down the street invited Colleen to church and Sunday school, her mother thought, *How good of them to include Colleen. Every child ought to go to Sunday school.* With an active young people's group, the Mormon church met social needs in Colleen's growing years. Its activities were wholesome and upright, stressing good works, and furthermore, it kept her busy. So as she grew older, Colleen considered herself a Mormon.

Drama was a natural for Colleen during high school. It

was fun to get under the skin of the character she was playing and project her likeness to the audience. Imaginative, exuberant and unaffected, she had a winsome freedom on the stage.

Exhilarated by the laughter and banter of rehearsals and the high excitement of the entire cast on opening night, Colleen thought of drama in much the same way a high school fellow might react to playing football. It was one of her extra-curricular activities. She hadn't planned that it should be more than that.

While a junior in high school, Colleen won a dramatic T.V. scholarship which led to a Warner Brothers contract. A scholarship was given to an outstanding boy and girl as a television workshop promotion idea. Colleen won the girl's scholarship which entitled her to tutoring for a year. During this time, as part of the training, she did bit parts for television. It wasn't much, Colleen says, but it was exciting at the time, and a gentle push in the direction of Hollywood and the movies.

At sixteen Colleen graduated from high school and enrolled in Brigham Young University in Utah. She hoped to major in Sociology and minor in Speech. Here, away from home and facing adulthood as students are urged to do, Colleen began to sort things out. What was life all about? She felt so restless. Was there something more in life that she was missing out on? She wasn't all *that* old, but she knew a kind of emptiness that was hard to describe to anyone else.

Hungry to know what that "something more" could be, Colleen felt she should stop just being a church attender and actually join the church. She did this, and began teaching a Sunday school class as well. Increasing her activity in the church didn't prove to be the answer, however. She found herself whirling around in "churchianity," not knowing what she was looking for and being kept too busy to find out any new direction for life. The church stressed good works, and Colleen filled her life doing them.

To earn money to help with her education, Colleen did

modeling occasionally for a photographer who was a family friend. The photographer was exceptionally skilled and the two of them worked well together.

He would occasionally come to the university with her mother and spend a day photographing Colleen — in the mountains in the snow, in the swimming pool, on the tennis courts — his casual out-of-doors shots captured Colleen's fresh, wholesome beauty. The natural charm of this kind of photograph was popular at the time, and out of one day's work, the photographer might sell four magazine covers — a downright unusual bit of success. If you were reading periodicals in the late 1940's, Colleen's face may have looked up at you when you dropped your favorite magazine on the sofa.

Eventually the girl on the covers was noticed by more than magazine publishers. Toward the end of her sophomore year someone at 20th Century-Fox Studios saw her pictures and was impressed. An invitation came for a screen test. An offer of a film contract with the studio followed.

It wasn't easy to decide. Colleen wanted a college education really more than anything else, but funds were low. The contract with 20th Century would alleviate this financial burden.

In the end Colleen dropped out of one school and was put into another. For six months she had classes in walking, talking, dancing, emoting and general orientation to the studio. At the end of this time she made additional screen tests and, after seeing them, the head producer called for an interview.

An eighteen-year-old girl's heart did some flip-flops as she went in. They had a part ready for her in a picture, he said, and proceeded to give her a look into the future that surpassed what she could have imagined.

"And yet," said Colleen, "as I stood there I had a terrible sinking feeling. I was thrilled and yet I knew at the same time that it wouldn't be enough. Here I was being offered more than I ever dreamed of — a wonderful part, money, fun — and still it wasn't enough. In a way, it was my moment of truth."

How devastating to realize that the best you thought life could offer still left a void!

But it was an exciting, creative life. It was also a heap of hard work. Colleen was caught up in the whirl of all she was learning and the new friends she met. She was not sorry about the choice she had made. She stayed with 20th Century-Fox for three years and during this time she played major roles in three pictures.

Her first leading role was in *The Walls of Jericho,* a wonderful part that she loved playing. Jericho was a typical small town infected with gossip which centered around a sixteen-year-old girl who had killed the town drunk during a scuffle with him when he had made advances toward her. The story climaxed in a grueling murder trial and her eventual acquittal. Colleen played the girl, and when she reminisces about the film it is obvious that she had fun playing this part.

Somewhere about this time Colleen met a young man she had known in high school. She went backstage after attending a play at Occidental College to congratulate the cast, and he was there with another group of old friends. His name was Louis Evans, Jr., a minister's son. He called her later to ask for a date, an invitation which he repeated fairly often.

The next summer Louis Evans went to a young people's conference in the mountains, and called Colleen the first night after he got home.

"I've got to talk to you," he said.

He told her what had happened to him and to some of the others in the group in the mountains, how the Spirit of God had spoken to them in a special way. Louis had always been a good guy, what you would expect of a minister's son, but not all that different from Colleen's other friends. But now he had something more — a radiance, a personal experience with Jesus Christ which he talked about. He left Colleen bewildered. She didn't understand at all what he was talking about. It scared and attracted her at the same time. She remembers thinking, "I don't know what he's got, but whatever it is, it is what I want."

Convinced that Colleen must know about this too, Louis brought Colleen into the friendship of that group of young people at Hollywood Presbyterian church in the weeks that followed. Many of them shared Louis' enthusiasm and gradually what they were saying began to get through to her. At another conference at summer's end, Colleen went with them.

She listened eagerly to all that was being said, filtering much of it through her past experiences. The concepts of the Saviourhood of Jesus Christ, and the need for redemption and faith were all falling into pre-conditioned boxes in her mind. How did one make sense out of all this? She could not deny what she saw in the lives of her new friends. It wasn't all crystal clear yet, but she knew in order to know God, she had to know Jesus Christ.

Unrest, a troubled heart sent her walking along the mountainside alone. She felt a heavy pressure inside her, as though God were urging her spirit. How strange that she should feel so irresistibly drawn to Him, yet so constrained to "figure it all out" before accepting His invitation. At last she knew she must capitulate to Jesus Christ. There was no other way.

She simply said to Him, "This is it. I want to say *yes* to You. I don't understand all that I'm doing, but I want *You*."

It wasn't much of a prayer, and it took some time for her to comprehend all that happened in that simple conversation with God. Christ entered her life and made His presence known. Peace came with giving herself to God. Her life seemed flooded with love — God's love. She *felt* loved — and this worked its way out in her relationships with other people.

Colleen became a member of the dynamic group at Hollywood Presbyterian Church which had so attracted her to

Jesus Christ. The fellowship there was a spiritually stimulating balance to her life at the studio, and the Christian training she was receiving was giving stability and direction to her life.

For two and a half more years she stayed on at 20th Century-Fox. The people with whom she was working were immensely interesting, and although she heard rumors of distasteful things, she never knew these personally in her Hollywood contacts. She *liked* these people; she enjoyed being with them. In retrospect Colleen sees that these years of relating Christ to this kind of a world were part of a valuable experience.

The last film she made in Hollywood was *Willy Comes Marching Home*. When she did leave it was not with a holier-than-thou attitude or a spirit of disdain. It was more beautifully what someone called "the expulsive power of a positive new affection."

"Hollywood is demanding and takes all you've got," says Colleen.

Public appearance tours became tiresome and were taking too much time. She wanted to be free to do Christian work and to accompany the young people from the church on deputation meetings. Attendance at good conferences was eliminated by studio responsibilities. "The tail was wagging the dog," Colleen concluded.

Twenty-one years old, Colleen left the studio and a blossoming career and enrolled in a liberal arts college to finish her education. Later she hoped to go on to seminary to prepare for Christian work. That is, until Louis Evans entered the picture again with a different proposal. During the first semester, he asked her to marry him.

The summer before their marriage Colleen made a Christian film, *Great Discovery,* and then went to Europe to participate in a work camp project sponsored by the World Council of Churches. Louis, who had just graduated from Occidental College, went to Germany to help build an orphan home under the same program. Colleen's assignment was to a camp for Baltic refugees outside of Paris.

Both wanted to expose themselves to a needy world and for both of them this was a significant experience in expressing Christ's love.

The wedding took place in December of 1950, and Louis and Colleen together attended seminary in San Francisco for the next three years. Those were growing years — growing together and growing in the Lord, a process which still continues. They traveled for the seminary doing deputation work, and the first summer they returned to Europe to help in a work camp in Italy.

Here Christians from the eastern zone, a motley mixture of communists and others were gathered into one place. Together they hammered out ideas and the reality of Christ in what proved to be anything but a sheltered situation. Colleen believes the experience has helped shape Louis' ministry and strengthened his belief that the Gospel must speak to the needs of a real and total world.

Following seminary Louis was given a grant to study in Edinburgh, Scotland, for two years. Colleen adjusted to the rigors of Scottish life — a cold-on-the-edges cottage, a culture with different values, more learning. Together they enjoyed the pleasure of it all. And part of the pleasure was the birth of a son.

Louis began preaching regularly in a small Scottish church. Later when the first Billy Graham London Crusade began, the Evans were key helpers. For a time Colleen continued to accept invitations to give her testimony and to do some Christian film work. Then their second son was born.

One day as she was leaving the house, she looked back to wave good-bye to Louis, who had generously planned to baby-sit. There he stood, holding the baby and its bottle. Life seemed so hectic, one or the other of them was always hurrying off somewhere. *Why am I doing this*? she thought. *Those babies and my husband are my life, not this*. That was the beginning of the end of accepting too much to do. The decks were cleared for real family life.

Back in the States the Evanses applied to the Board of Ecumenical Missions for a mission post in Africa. No openings were on the horizon and they were turned down. Being refused had never occurred to them!

The Presbytery of Los Angeles suggested a post they wanted the Evanses to accept, however. They asked them to begin a mission church in Bel Air, California. A far cry from the mission field, they thought. Looking the situation over, they drove through the area, readjusted their thinking, sought the will of God, and said *yes*. They moved into a new home and began work.

It was a somewhat disappointing assignment, they thought at first. They had planned to be sacrificial and take a hard post overseas. *Here we are in Bel Air, California,* thought Colleen, *in a lovely house, in a beautiful area, in the middle of our own culture. No hardship in this.* But hardships come in different shapes, Colleen was soon to find out.

Baby number three (a darling girl) arrived, and then number four (another son). The house was the church meeting place, she seldom saw her busy husband, and the front room was regularly full of people. Colleen felt akin to a sinking ship. "O, help, Lord!" became a fairly regular cry of desperation.

Overtired most of the time, she was grappling with life as the mother of four children (four in five years) and the wife of an extremely active man. Added to this she was really the church custodian by virtue of the church meeting place, and she was still feeling pressured into accepting too many outside responsibilities. Sometimes she felt like she was caught in an egg-beater. Bursting into tears and feeling cross were the painful side effects.

Colleen came face to face with Colleen and had a good look at herself. Being a professional Christian was being a phoney. She must be a Christian at home first of all. What she was to these babies and to her husband was what really counted. She decided to try to be what God wanted her to be, not what others thought she should be.

"I took an honest look at myself. I was tired of being an 'image' Christian. I wanted to be a real Christian."

Today Colleen tells others young mothers what she early learned. "For God's sake, say *no.* Take the criticism of people and groups but be a faithful mother and wife. If a woman is fortunate enough to be a wife and a mother, that's her career. It's a ministry of *intangibles."*

Since the time of the honest look, Colleen accepts only one appointment a month. Her husband is gone away from home much of the time and she feels strongly about her role of "holding the home" while he is gone. One parent must provide the stability for the children simply by being there and ready to listen. She says,

"We will all make mistakes with our child-raising because we are human, but let's not do it by default."

The Evanses found the work in Bel Air more rewarding than they dreamed it could be. Starting a church from scratch took some doing. Louis Evans believes in building men. He began looking for men who were open to learn and capable of leading others. He made it a policy to invest heavily in a few, to encourage them to think Biblically, to study and then to reach out to others. Each of the men he trains eventually prepares his own curriculum of study and later trains a similar group in the church program for study and outreach.

Louis and Colleen knew how inspiring the love and fellowship of a small group could be to devout Christian living. They began encouraging what they called *Nurture* groups — small groups, usually in neighborhoods, where people could study together, freely share their doubts and discouragements as well as what Christ was teaching them. To these small sharing groups and the training of leaders, the Evanses attribute the phenomenal growth of the Bel Air church. The genuine Christian experience of all who joined the group gave the church unity and power.

One day Louis commented to Colleen, "God has blessed this work so much and raised up such capable leaders that we could leave and the work would go on without us."

Shortly thereafter, the Evanses received a call to the large Presbyterian Church of La Jolla, California, where they presently minister. They are attempting to put the same principles into practice in an already well-established church.

When Louis married Colleen he got himself a wife as creative and courageous as he. Louis' words, "Let's be slaves of Christ, not of men," have led them to take strong stands on social isues, which are sometimes painful. The Evanses keep remembering that Christians are salt and light, and that both of these hurt sometimes.

Colleen is not a "managing" minister's wife. Her life is open to others, and she speaks honestly about her needs and experiences with Christ.

"She does not know *strangers,"* Dr. Evans' secretary says. "Everyone is a friend to Colleen."

And this is important in an area where much of the population is mobile and often includes families from overseas whose fathers are highly trained in scientific fields and come to one of the many important industries in La Jolla.

Others, observing her simple graciousness and genuineness in the Lord, have been stimulated to rethink their own Christian commitment or challenged to show the kind of love that seems to flow so naturally from Colleen because she is in touch with the Source of Love.

This love of Colleen's makes her a good listener to troubled people and arouses once-dead hope in some who are in despair. It also brings home almost many unexpected dinner guests, and a flurry of telephone calls.

But *loving* is what Colleen feels called to be. She found out quite a while ago that she couldn't manage this under her own steam or with any stage techniques. She would have to have help from Outside. Now she no longer strives to love. The secret is in spending time with the Lord in fellowship and prayer so that He can do the loving through her.

The pace of life has changed as small-sized Evanses have become medium-sized. Dinner time these days at the Evans' home with four interesting, strong-minded children is sometimes riotous. Discussions are so high-powered the children actually raise their hands to bid for a turn to speak. Colleen says, "Louis is a direct, honest, stimulating man who really makes things move, and his children respond to the lead!"

The Evanses work at making Saturday a family day. If they must take a trip, they usually try to take one of their children with them, even if this means taking them out of school. The extra expense of this is budgeted out because they think this time alone with one child is so important.

"They are all close in age, and each needs to be treated as an individual, not as 'the children,' " Colleen adds. "Each gets a turn, and the occasions become special treats."

Praying together about the details of each one's life, as well as Biblical instruction are foundations of their home. They want the *children* as well as the congregation to think Biblically. In keeping with the Evanses emphasis on Christ in the world, the children are encouraged to find Christian answers to the world's problems. Reading aloud from both classics and appropriate modern bestsellers is a favorite family affair, enjoyed especially on vacations.

Colleen does not take organizational responsibilities in the church or elsewhere, preferring to be free to be the friend in need to people along the way. Some week it may be a run-away girl who needs her friendship, another time a woman on the verge of a nervous breakdown. With each Colleen wants to share what God has taught her about Himself. A self-giving ministry demands fellowship with a living Lord, and that, too, takes time.

I like Colleen Evans because she is frankly excited about knowing God better. When she is asked to speak now, it is not because she was once a movie star. Instead, she is asked to give Biblical teaching from a book of the Bible. She has something to say because God has said it first to her.

Credit for her spiritual growth goes to her husband, Colleen is quick to say. "He has made me face myself and pushed me to be an honest, growing person. When I've been tempted to be what others thought I should be, he has been quick to say, 'You be yourself, Cokie. Be what God wants you to be.' And, of course, it was seeing the change in his life in the first place that made me hungry to know Jesus Christ."

It has been eighteen years since a lovely young girl first realized that life couldn't produce enough thrills to satisfy her basic longings. Nothing has been the same since she has come to know Christ.

Not that life is always easy. She often feels the pressure of people and knows an awful weariness. Leading a large congregation has some built-in heartaches, and being a minister's wife can be a lonely road. But that's not the point. It's knowing God that makes the difference. Imagine being able to say, "I know God!"

19

Edith Edman

Edith Edman is known to many Wheaton College graduates as "Friend Wife" as her husband, V. Raymond Edman, now Chancellor of Wheaton College, has lovingly referred to her over the years. Edith Edman has a large capacity for knowing God, and He has taken her from the shallows into the wonders of the deep places, as she has opened up her life to Him.

EDITH EDMAN is one of God's noble women. Attractive and warm-hearted, and now in her sixties, this woman has an inner source of vitality flowing out of her life which brings refreshment to all who know her. She puts life in focus. You forget the woes of your human predicament and see God instead.

Then you might think, as others have, *I wish I could be like that.* As if wishing could make an instantaneous miracle happen that would give depth of character and inner beauty. Or, as if some people have all the breaks and are born that way. No, Edith Edman has become this way over years of fellowship and dynamic encounter with God. There are no short-cuts.

Edith began with a goodly heritage, however; her mother and father loved God. From the time she was ten years old, a devout home environment was supplemented by summers spent at Old Orchard, Maine, where Dr. A. B. Simpson began a conference ministry. Dr. Simpson had left the complexities of an old-line denomination and in the woods of Maine began this fellowship to minister to hungry hearts. Two major insights were given to him over the years. One was a vision of the holiness of God; the other was a vision of missions. Out of the conference site at Old Orchard, the Christian and Missionary Alliance Church came into being.

The teaching of this great man of God, his emphasis on God's holiness, and his missionary spirit, was a great influence in the life of a young girl named Edith Olson. When she was thirteen years old, overwhelmed by her great sinfulness, Edith asked Jesus Christ to forgive her sins and make her His own. While other teen-agers in this resort area of Maine found hilarity and release at dances and movies, this pretty brown-eyed girl with the eager, open face found her satisfaction at the conference meetings. Missionaries from all over the world came to Old Orchard to tell what they had seen God do in strange lands. And Edith drank it in.

When she was seventeen, Edith gave her life to God for foreign missionary service. She remembers the occasion so clearly. She happened to be standing by their old-fashioned ice box when a phrase of a conference hymn came to her mind, "I would walk alone with Jesus . . ." She told Him then that she would go wherever He sent.

Looking back on this decision now, Edith Edman calls it the beginning of genuine commitment. She believes young people have a great capacity for God if they really give themselves to Him. She recounts how at twenty years of age Jonathan Edwards wrote his seventy resolves with God, and how the last of these was a resolve "to have a spirit of gentleness." Jim Elliott's diary at the age of twenty-three reveals profound dealings with God.

Sometime between then and the completion of her training for the mission field, V. Raymond Edman came into Edith's life. He sailed for Ecuador shortly after his graduation from Boston University. A year later she was also in that little South American republic and they were married in its capital city of Quito.

Before another year had passed, however, her husband almost died of typhus and they had to return to the States for eighteen months' recuperation. Again they returned to Ecuador where Mr. Edman began a Bible school for their mission. This time he was stricken with dengue and amoebic dysentery. He became so weak that he often taught classes from his bed. When no improvement came, it was decided that he must return to the States for medical care. Edith would remain in Ecuador with Roland, the younger of their two small sons. Mr. Edman would take the older boy, Charles, home with him.

Alone in the port city of Guayaquil, Edith faced her tremendous need of God. Walking through the streets, surveying the colossal needs all around her, she felt like she was drowning. What could she do, one missionary alone, a young mother with a child? What *was* she doing? The odds were so evident and so crushing. Disappointment, dejection, discouragement. She was on the skids to defeat. Back in her room, she went before God and asked for a fresh anointing of His Holy Spirit. She determined she would not leave the room until God came and proved His reality and His adequacy.

Edith Edman knows He came to her that day. Things have looked different and been different since that day. She said, "He showed me it was His work, not mine, and I had only to rest in His power and faithfulness." Her panicky concern was gone; God was the answer. Instead of drowning in despair, Edith was overwhelmed by God.

The next day, almost as if to solidify a new plateau of faith in an earnest disciple, God did a special thing for Edith. She was asked to go to see a dying woman who had been active in the Ecuadorian church. Still living in the glow of

God's touch on her life, Edith prayed with the woman and had the audacity to ask God to heal her. And God answered.

American physicians would not give Raymond Edman medical clearance to return to the tropics, so Edith came home with Roland. This wasn't at all what they had planned. How could it possibly not be God's will to be in Ecuador when that was where they wanted to be so much! Then they remembered that they had told God they would go "anywhere" for Him. He sent them to a tiny Alliance church in Worcester, Massachusetts. Twenty-five people showed up for the first morning worship service; six for the evening service. Not exactly inspiring, but the will of God for the Edmans.

But God had a bigger plan in mind in sending them there. One mile away was Clark University and Raymond enrolled for course work on a Ph.D. program. He worked hard in the church and gave his people good spiritual food, so the congregation grew and the church prospered. A daily radio program opened up an opportunity for both ministry and valuable experience.

Edith was now twenty-nine the mother of three small children, and confined to the home much of the time. Somewhere she came upon a copy of the *Memoirs of McCheyne*. As she waded through this book, she began to have a hunger to see revival come to the church of Jesus Christ. Robert McCheyne had yearned for revival in his church in Scotland, and throughout the book runs the strong thread of his faith that God would move among the people in a fresh way. Edith was stirred. McCheyne had died at twenty-nine, and here she was already twenty-nine and she had not entered into such dealings of faith as this man had. How much did she care about God's church? So Edith told God, "I would see a mighty stirring of God in my lifetime as McCheyne did." And she began to pray to that end.

Her first move was to begin a women's prayer meeting in the church. This was an unheard of idea, but the women were carried along with Edith's enthusiasm and agreed to meet. But on the day of the prayer meeting, only one other woman showed up. Edith gulped down her disappointment, especially when the other woman said, "What's the use?" and kept a positive attitude. She told the woman they met the scriptural requirement of two or three gathered in His name. They prayed together, not with great faith, but at least they prayed. The next week six women came. In the weeks to come women, hungry for God, came from other churches to join them, and today many of them have a deep ministry of prayer. Ever since that first prayer meeting, wherever Edith has gone she has begun a women's prayer meeting. And always in her heart was this urgent desire to see God move in His church — revival!

After six years as a pastor, the Edmans went to Nyack, New York where Dr. Edman joined the faculty of the Nyack Missionary Training School. At home, Edith prayed for revival, thinking perhaps it would come to the students at Nyack. Often when Dr. Edman came home from chapel services she would ask, "Is there any sign of God's working in an unusual way?" Why did she persist so intensely in this prayer? Edith believes God put it on her heart continually, even though she was a young mother with small children and many distractions. She knew that sometime in her lifetime, God would let her see the answer to her prayer.

Years later in 1943, when Dr. Edman had become president of Wheaton College, God did visit Wheaton College to revive the students. Concern for personal holiness, for a right relationship with God and others, broke out all over the campus. Revival had come. One night after Dr. Edman had finished praying with a freshman boy who had just received Christ, he turned to find another young man who wanted to transact some important business with God waiting for a talk with him. That young man's name was Billy Graham.

Tears spilled out of Mrs. Edman's eyes as she shared this special gift from God with me. "To think," she said, "that God would put a desire like this on a young mother's heart, and then let her live to see how He answered. Why, Billy has touched kings and presidents for God."

I've always had the feeling when I've been with Edith

Edman that she was a friend of God. She has shared the great concern on the heart of God for years. She has cared; and that is what a friend does.

Since that time the Edmans' children have grown, and Edith has more time to pray. In 1950 when God stirred the lives of Wheaton students again, He also worked in Edith's heart. He reworked her set of values and asked her to be His disciple in a special way. She saw His holiness in a new experience, and saw how shabby some of her choice treasures were. She determined to spend more time with God, and He has given her a ministry of intercession.

Retired now from the heavy duties of the presidency, Dr. Edman joins his wife in this ministry. Early in the morning the Edmans rise to talk to God about the things He places on their hearts. This is no pious performance to gain merit in His sight. The Edmans simply feel this is the ministry God has given them in these years. He has asked them to do this, and their obedience has brought them great delight. Obedience always does this, says Edith. Four-thirty is no longer early enough because the times goes so rapidly. There is so much to talk with Him about, and says Edith, "We wouldn't miss this fellowship for anything."

And it does cost. Wheaton, so full of good, inspiring things to attend and interesting people to know, hears the Edmans refuse invitations for the late evenings. There are just some things you can't do and still rise early alert enough to talk with God intelligently.

"What do you pray about?" I asked.

"How does that John Newton hymn in the *Inter-Varsity Hymns* go?" she asked in return. I repeated the words:

> Thou art coming to a King,
> Large petitions with thee bring;
> For His grace and power are such,
> None can ever ask too much.

"That's it," she said, and then went on to tell me how God has led them to pray for great things — for governments, for rulers, for an outpouring of His Spirit on the church, for answers to political crises in various countries of the world which affect the progress of the church. They pray for South Vietnam, for stability in national leadership, for Vietnamese soldiers and families, for national pastors and the national church. They ask God for wisdom for our State Department, for the president and his advisors, for our American soldiers, for missionaries. And they pray for people.

An enlarged heart has an enlarged vision. The reason most people pray so small is because they see so small, and their God is too small. Edith Edman's values have changed. She has a heart as big as the world and a God big enough to meet its needs.

One of God's recent good gifts to Edith Edman was to allow her to accompany her husband on a return trip to Ecuador. Dayuma, the well-known Auca Indian convert, had organized a work party to clear the jungle to allow the small Missionary Aviation Fellowship plane to land near the Auca village and bring in the Edmans. Dr. Edman gave Bible instruction and conducted the first Lord's supper for the believers in this tribe, ten years after the five missionaries who sought to reach them with God's message had been killed on the beach of the Curaray River. Most of these missionaries had been graduates of Wheaton College and dear to the Edmans.

Now here they were sitting under the thatched roof, on grass mats, in the middle of the jungle, seeing the fruit of the Gospel in the lives of a stone-age tribe. Personal faith in Jesus Christ has revolutionized the lives of people who had known only fear and hate. They, who had no concept of a tribal chief, of love, of holiness, now are children of a Heavenly Chief and know how to love each other because they know God's love and have been made righteous through personal faith in His Son. *This is the miracle of faith,* thought Edith Edman.

Mrs. Edman said that as she listened to their two-note music, as they sang original songs of endless verses, telling of God's redemption, she thought how flabby and short-sighted our civilized values are. These people were in on the only Reality. In simplicity, they knew God. No pretense, no sophistication. As she listened to their testimonies, interpreted for them by Rachael Saint, she thought, "I'm going to live in heaven forever with these dear people and I'm glad."

Later she watched as Dr. Edman baptized eleven new believers in the river, and then commissioned two of the men, both involved in the missionary killing, to go as missionaries to reach the downriver group of Aucas with the message of God's love. Much had happened in Ecuador and in the life of Edith Edman since that day when she left to rejoin her husband in the States and thought her career as a missionary had ended.

This is not all of Edith Edman's story. It says nothing of the details of her life as the college president's wife, of the outreach of her friendships, of her speaking ministry, of her role as the mother of four sons. She has had her heartaches and discouraging moments like everyone else. But they have been put into perspective by the three major encounters with God that have been recounted here.

She asked to see the glory of God, and God has been pleased to reveal Himself to her in a deep way. She has a large capacity for God because she opened her life to Him without fearing what it might mean to have Him really come in. The imprint of His life is on hers.

★ ★

I have kept Edith Edman's story until last because you might not have understood if you had met her first. Fellowship with God does lead into a big life — too big for those who prefer the confining circumference of self.

It is a risky thing to open up your life to God, with no private corners for self, but only those who do ever find out why they exist and what forgiveness, love, peace and joy mean. None of us will ever get a further glimpse of God's holiness and the splendor of knowing Him unless we really want *Him* more than any other thing or person. While we hold our tawdry prizes tightly in our hands, He offers each of us the glory of a friendship with the eternal God.

Epilogue

My dear Lord, Jesus Christ,
I pray Thee for Thy help, lest I forget
When I should most remember,
Those times when, in Thy swift redeeming passage on this earth,
The radiance of Thy special grace,
Sought out a woman.
To be mankind's first witness to some wonder yet unknown —
Impress upon my mind how
Tho' Son of God, a woman bore Thee;
How Thy first miracle,
When words changed water into wine at Cana,
Was wrought to grant a woman's plea;
How the Samaritan,
Who gave Thee water from her alien well,
Was first to learn from Thee Thy wondrous Name:
How a woman with a broken heart,
Who sought Thy broken body in the tomb,
Was first to hear Thy voice again, after the Cross,
And, startled by the light of Thee,
Was shown the prophecy fulfilled!
From Thee each one received a first-fruit of Thy tree;
First sound of life,
First miracle,
First revelation of Thyself, Messiah,
First proof that Death, in Thee, could have no part.
With true humility, dear Lord, I pray:
Make me to be a woman worthy of the name,
With courage, born of love, to follow Thee,
Not just in wish or thought, which are unseen,

But in my every act the world can see.
And give me Love, dear Lord,
That at my end when my own dawn is rising
I, too, like Mary at the tomb,
May, of a sudden, know that Thou art there,
Calling my name as Thou didst hers
Before the break of day.

—*Lisa Sergio* "Lest We Forget"[1]

---

[1]From *Prayers of Women* by Lisa Sergio. Used by permission of Harper & Row, Publishers, Inc.